Docilitas

Laches: But I am astonished that you are inviting us to be your fellow counsellors in the education of the young men and are not inviting Socrates here! In the first place, he comes from your own deme, and in the second, he is always spending his time in places where the young men engage in any study or noble pursuit of the sort you are looking for.

Lysimachus: What do you mean, Laches? Has our friend Socrates concerned himself with any things of this kind?

Laches: Certainly, Lysimachus.

Nicias: This is a point I can vouch for no less than Laches, since he only recently recommended a man to me as a music teacher for my son. — Plato, *Laches*, (180c–d).

Learning things and wondering at things are also pleasant as a rule; wondering implies the desire of learning, so that the object of wonder is an object of desire; while in learning one is brought into one's natural condition. — Aristotle, *Rhetoric*, I, 11 (1371a31–32).

Similarly you as well as other men who judge matters suitably would reply to a garrulous word-lover who said: "I teach in order to talk" with "Man, why not rather speak in order to teach?" For if these things are true, as you know they are, you truly see how much less words are to be esteemed than that for the sake of which we use words, since the use of words is superior to the words. For words exist in order that they may be used, and in addition we use them in order to teach. As teaching is superior to talking, in like degree speech is better than words. So of course doctrine is far superior to words. — Augustine, "On the Teacher", c. 9

Looking back on a wild and wasted life, I realize that I have especially sinned in neglecting to read novels. I mean the really novel novels; for such old lumber as Dickens and Jane Austen I know fairly well. If instead of trifling away my time over pamphlets about Collectivism or Co-operation, plunging for mere pleasure into the unhealthy excitement of theological debates with dons, or enjoying the empty mirth of statistics about Poland and Czechoslovakia, I had quietly sat at home doing my duty and reading every novel as it came out, I might be a more serious and earnest man than I am today . . . . (Still) the old literature, both great and trivial, was built on the idea that there is a purpose in life, even if it is not always completed in this life; and it really was interesting to follow the stages of such a purpose . . .

— G. K. Chesterton, "*On Philosophy* versus *Fiction*",
All Is Grist (1931).

Our mind is unable to know itself in such a way that it immediately apprehends itself, but it arrives at knowledge of itself by the fact that it perceives other things.   — Aquinas, *De Veritate*, 10, 8.

Other St. Augustine's Press books from James Schall
The Regensburg Lecture
Sum Total of Human Happiness
Remembering Belloc
The Praise of "Sons of Bitches"
On the Principles of Taxing Beer:
And Other Brief Philosophical Essays
The Modern Age
The Classical Moment

Introductions or selections from James Schall
Josef Pieper, *What Does "Academic" Mean?*
Josef Pieper, *The Platonic Myths*
Marc Guerra, *Liberating Logos*
Marc Guerra, *Jerusalem, Athens, and Rome*

Docilitas
On Teaching and Being Taught

James v. Schall

ST. AUGUSTINE'S PRESS
South Bend, Indiana

Manufactured in the United States of America.

1 2 3 4 5 6   22 21 20 19 18 17 16

Library of Congress Cataloging in Publication Data
Schall, James V.
Docilitas: on teaching and being taught / James V. Schall.
pages cm
Includes index.
ISBN 978-1-58731-182-6 (hardback)
1. College teaching. 2. College teaching – Philosophy.
3. Education – Philosophy. 4. Reflective teaching. I. Title.
LB2331.S34 2015
378.1'25 – dc23   2015005661

∞ The paper used in this publication meets the minimum requirements of the American National Standard for Information Sciences – Permanence of Paper for Printed Materials, ANSI Z39.48-1984.

ST. AUGUSTINE'S PRESS
www.staugustine.net

Table of Contents

Acknowledgments

Chapters 1, 8, and 11, Ignatius Insight on-line.

Chapters 3, 4, 7, and 12, *Vital Speeches*.

Chapter 9, *New Blackfriars*.

Chapter 15, Catholic World Report.

Chapters 16, *Utraque Unum*.

Conclusion, *University Bookman*.

Introduction

KNOWLEDGE IS NOT "OWNED"

In the initial page of this book, I have cited short passages from Plato, Aristotle, Augustine, Chesterton, and Aquinas. Each of these selections taught me much. Each incited my attention to something that I probably never would have realized without their words. From the Laches of Plato, we find the young man who wants to "engage in any study or noble pursuits." In spite of his protestations that he is not a sophist—not, as he says, a teacher—Socrates will still recommend a man who can teach us music, itself a step to the highest things.

Aristotle is our immediate source for "wonder," for what incites our thinking, though Socrates often speaks of it. Aristotle tells us that learning and wondering are delights, which we have ourselves to experience so that we will recognize them. He tells us that this very wonder implies a "desire" to learn. Even more profoundly, he tells us that "the object of wonder is an object of desire." We are not locked only into ourselves.

Augustine even writes a short treatise "On the Teacher." In this dialogue, he seeks to instruct his own son, Adeodatus. Augustine knows about "garrulous word-lovers." We do not talk just to talk, but to speak the truth, even to "teach" it. The words we use, important as they are, stand for that to which they refer. Teaching is "superior" to just "talking," Augustine tells us. We look for "doctrine," the truth of things, not just words. We wish to converse, to speak. This conversation is what binds us to each other. Things also exist to be spoken about, to be learned about.

Chesterton is always amusing and always profound. For me, he stands for the fact that both amusement and profundity belong to the same truth. In the passage that I cited, he tells us about what he calls "old literature." He mentions Dickens and Jane Austen. He quips that he may be "trifling" his time away by "plunging, for mere pleasure, into the unhealthy excitement of theological debates with dons." This explanation sounds very much like Socrates on the Sophists. But Chesterton does tell us that the purpose of "the old literature, both great and trivial, was built on the idea that there is a purpose to life." He adds that this purpose may not always be "completed in this life." Literature follows the stages, from life to death, of this purpose of our lives as manifest in the way we actually live.

Finally, we have one sentence from Aquinas. He tells us what we need first to know. We do not know directly our own minds. But this does not mean that we know nothing of ourselves. He adds that we arrive at this knowledge of ourselves by first perceiving "other things." We become aware of ourselves when we know what we are not. I like to put it this way: We are given the gift of knowing ourselves by knowing first what is not ourselves. In other words, we do not first teach. We are first taught. We begin, as it were, in weakness, not power. Once we know this beginning, we have a chance of knowing what the mind is, the power given to us to know *all that is.*

A few years after I began teaching at Georgetown University, I published a short essay in the student newspaper, *The Hoya.* The essay was entitled, "What a Student Owes His Teacher." Subsequently, it was a central chapter in my book, *Another Sort of Learning.* This essay became generally popular, usually found on internet. In comments and letters, many students and teachers over the years told me that they had never quite looked on the fact that a student "owes" the teacher anything, let alone the discipline and the attention necessary to carry out the project of teaching so that others might learn. Moreover, something else was needed, not merely the good will of the student but his willingness to do the sometimes hard work of learning. This latter necessity no professor could give a student. This willingness is what I will call, to use the Latin expression, *docilitas.* We have the same word in English, docility.

As a course progresses through a semester or a year, this willingness to be taught should rouse in the student something more. He should find in his soul a conscious desire to learn, a fascination with the whole enterprise, a sense that something exists out there that he wants to know. Indeed, in learning we should experience a genuine "pleasure," the lack of which is ultimately devastating to the student enterprise. This excitement and delight are not things that a teacher can "give" to a student. It has to come from within the student's own soul.

It is true that a professor's enthusiasm may be catching and lead to imitation. But I had in mind something more. At the end of a course, a student ought to walk away satisfied that he learned something. But he is still fully aware that much is still there to know, deeper, more profoundly. He now is "unsatisfied." He is at least aware of the vast reaches of *what is*, about which he knows little or nothing. In true Socratic fashion, it is refreshing to know that we do not know even when we do know something. We are left with a desire to know more of what is to be known, which is, ultimately, *all that is*.

In recent years, I have had the opportunity to address many different audiences about teaching, learning, within the context of academic life and in the sphere of general learning. But in a number of my books, including *Another Sort of Learning*, I have tried to do something further. I have become concerned with the student who, even in the best and most prestigious of universities, or just anywhere in or out of academia, has not known where to go when he is aware that something is lacking to him. He does not want just to "get an education," as it is somewhat awkwardly put. He seeks the truth of things. We are surrounded by a culture of relativism and skepticism about the knowing mind. It need not be so that we simply accept it as all there is.

Of late, I have also had an opportunity to speak of teaching. This topic, of course, is the co-relative theme for a student who seeks to learn. The student and teacher are locked in the same world. If I might put it that way, the teacher does not "teach" and the learner does not "learn." Rather both student and teacher address the same world in which they both exist. *Knowledge is not "owned"* by the teacher, nor is it "purchased" by the student's tuition. It is not a commodity, not that there is anything wrong with commodities.

Knowledge is free. A student, having learned something, does not walk away on the last day of class with something of the professor's brain. The professor retains his brain, such as it is, though few good academics fail to learn something while teaching their students. The only thing a professor can do is bring the student to see something he, the professor, does not own or simply concoct by himself, though sharp students can usually suspect when a professor is doing something unsupported by truth. When both student and teacher see the truth of something, both can rest and rejoice over something greater than either, something *that is* that both can praise for its own sake.

A professor is not wise to be a proud man in that Augustinian sense of *superbia*, of thinking that he himself is the cause of the truth of things. He is, at best, also someone who receives what is there, *what is*. At bottom, the world is gift-oriented. The student-teacher relationship is, in some ways, necessarily ephemeral. At the end of each semester, I confess a certain poignancy. I watch my two classes, with from sixty to a hundred students each. One by one, each leaves the room for the last time. Chances of ever seeing most again are pretty slim. Each student has his own life to live. You are at best a guide, hopefully a good one.

As we learn from experience, we will see very few of these students again. They are off to their own lives. And that is the way it should be. I have often been consoled by Chesterton's remark on the difference between a mother and a teacher. A teacher, he said, teaches one thing to a hundred students, while a mother teaches a hundred things to one child. I have, I confess, often tried to make students also aware of the hundred things, perhaps even of the "hundred-fold" of which Scripture speaks. As in the Appendix to this book, I want to leave them with things yet to read, things they would likely not come by in ordinary life.

When a student first walks into my class, of course, he has

already lived with his parents for eighteen or nineteen years. When he graduates some four years later, he has to find his way in the world. The important things will still be there for him to choose and live by, or, yes, to reject and still live by the rejection. Professors can hope that they did not neglect to speak of the highest things, the important things, *the things that are.*

Professors are glad that they did not lie to the students or, as Plato said, did not lie to themselves, about *what is.* But too, they hope that they have warned them that they can betray their own lives, if they choose. They can miss what is important. Universities provide a hundred ways to help students in this latter way if they want to find them. What we know involves a choice about what we want to know. I first read that admonition in Aristotle and have often thanked him for its wisdom.

This book, following *Another Sort of Learning*, is for me a second look at liberal education and teaching, at reading and knowing. I find that I have had occasion to speak in many ways to different kinds of audiences about these learning and teaching endeavors. I have brought them together here to see them all at once. None of these collected lectures and essays is overly solemn. There is a lightsomeness about them, as there is about life itself. We ourselves do not exist by "necessity." As I have remarked, a teacher is often tempted to be an entertainer, a song and dance man. But if he has none of this entertainment syndrome in his bones, he can hardly be a good teacher. Not much goes on in a classroom when no laughter is found in it.

My, now lengthy, experience with being a professor, however, teaches me that the academic vocation is often filled with the highest of delights. A student solemnly comes up to you. He wants to know whether a Christian can agree with Nietzsche. You have just told the class that you rather like Nietzsche. You are not surprised at the number of students who choose to write their short paper on Aristotle on friendship. You smile. You wrote on the same topic too about their age and later when you were supposed to be more mature. Friendship is the greatest of all human topics, even reaching to the divinity.

The title of this book, as I said, is the Latin word *Docilitas*. Do not be frightened by it. It is a great word. I have put its meaning in the sub-title: "on being taught." Or even better, the emphasis should be on one's openness, on one's delight, in being taught. How much more wonderful it really is to learn things that are true from a good professor who, as you somehow suspect, knows what he is talking about. I was fortunate to have a number of these teachers in my youth and more as friends in my later years.

Something engages us in the pursuit of wisdom, something that arises from the human conversation that seeks the truth. Socrates, the philosopher, when we know him, leaves an indelible impression on all who encounter him. As I often say, there is no such thing as a university in which constant teaching of Plato is not going on. This Platonic reference will often appear in these pages. Usually, if we get to Plato, we have a chance to get to everything else that makes a difference. But Plato himself cautions us on being exposed to things too early in life, even to himself.

I have thought to leave much of the flavor of the original lectures in these pages. In *Another Sort of Learning*, a chapter is entitled: "On Lectures." Something important happens when human beings speak to and listen to each other. When invited, they speak what they want to say. Audience listens to what is said. A lecture, at its best, includes the thinking about what one wants to say, about how to say it, to whom. A formal lecture is given to a set audience at a set time in a set place by an invited speaker.

And yet, we can read the lectures and sermons of the ancients. Once given, they still seek an audience. One of the mysteries of writing anything, I once read, is that you never know who, if anyone, will ever read it. Nor does a lecturer really know if those in the audience are listening. Yet, it is this hope that someone reads, that someone hears, that makes human life social. We not only want to say what we think is true; we want to hear it, read it also.

Rightly it is said that the highest things only exist in conversation. They only exist when someone knows them and knows that he does. We seek to know and to tell others what we know. But this involves listening to them. In both speaker and listener, there must be something in addition, the awareness that truth is first a gift to both. This speaking and listening is, I think, what this book is about. It is about libraries, reading rooms, teaching, and learning. In short, it is about our "teachability," about our willingness to be taught. We must admit that we first must want to know before we can actually know. And when we actually know, we can only really know something if it is true. For this knowing we are given a mind and we rejoice in it.

Chapter 1
PATRON SAINT OF TEACHERS*

Your total ignorance of that which you profess to teach merits the death penalty. I doubt whether you would know that St. Cassian of Imola was stabbed to death by his students with their styli. His death, a martyr's honorable one, made him a patron saint of teachers.
— Ignatius Reilly, in John Kennedy Toole, *A Confederacy of Dunces*.[1]

I.

'Tis well, at times, to think of the perplexing lot of the teacher. I had not known that a "patron saint" of teachers existed. And if there was one, I presumed, at least for the college and graduate crowd, that it was Augustine or Thomas Aquinas. Augustine, as we noted earlier, wrote a treatise "On the Teacher." In it, he taught his own son, Adeodatus, how to think about thinking of things.

Aquinas, even though he spent a good deal of time dealing with beginners, is usually considered better adapted to the more heady philosophical types. We know that Aquinas was not a martyr, even though he died rather young in 1274, at the age of 49. He left several unfinished works, including the famous *Summa Theologiae*. Augustine, busy in Hippo correcting the errors found in his vast earlier writings, just missed being a martyr. He died before the Van-

---

* This essay was originally written on-line for the beginning of the Second Semester, 2008, at Ignatius Insight.
1 John Kennedy Toole, *A Confederacy of Dunces* (New York: Grove Wedenfeld, 1980), p. 146.

dals managed to breech the walls of Hippo Regius in northern Africa in 430 A.D.

When I returned to Washington after family Christmas in California one year, I wanted a book to read on the Alaska Airlines Flight #6 from LAX to Reagan National. My niece lives some twenty minutes from LAX. Among the books on her shelves, I spotted John Kennedy Toole's *A Confederacy of Dunces*, a title from Swift. I began to read this novel during the summer but only covered a few pages. My niece let me have it to read on the five-hour flight to D.C. Since the Introduction was by Walker Percy, I figured it would be a pretty good read.

Somewhere over the eastern United States, I came to the passage that I cited above, about St. Cassian of Imola, the patron of teachers. Needless to say, I had not heard of St. Cassian before, at least not this one. As I recall, another Cassian, a medieval abbot, wrote something called *The Spiritual Meadow*, which, among other things, contains a number of amusing monastic anecdotes. So I looked up Cassian of Imola (a town near Ravenna) on Google. I found a reference to his Feast Day, August 13, from *Butler's Lives of the Saints.*

Cassian comes from the time of Julian the Apostate, in the fourth century A.D. or so. It seems that the Emperor had ordered all teachers to take an oath to the local gods, which Cassian, good Christian that he was, refused to do. (Our modern teachers take an implicit oath that they will not refer to any gods, pagan or Christian—something known as "free speech"). Roman soldiers who were Christian had the same problem. It was a local form of swearing loyalty to the state which was identified with the gods. To Christians, it seemed like state-supported blasphemy, which it was.

Cassian was evidently a stalwart professor who refused to make such an unjust oath. The local magistrate promptly decided to make an example of him. Cunning man that he was, the official involved the man's own students in his punishment. The students, not having finished the course, evidently had no problem with this strange form of justice. Cassian was stripped and tied to a post. From whence, his students, mindful of the man's punishments for their own scholarly laxities, drew their iron styli, pens used to mark on wax tablets, and stabbed the man to death.

So here we have it. A Christian teacher was stabbed to death, under state orders, by his own students with their own writing instruments for refusing to offer sacrifices to pagan gods. Today we have a more cruel punishment: we do not grant tenure to such stubborn types! But what could be a more graphic example for the scholarly vocation! One shudders to think of the varied lessons that students may draw from this account of how to deal with teachers!

In recording this remarkable history, the famous Butler, who wrote all the lives of the saints, laconically remarks: "There is no record of his (St. Cassian's) becoming a patron of teachers in spite of his pre-eminent qualifications for the role." Well, from now on, he is my man.

Recently, I decided to forbid computers from being used in my classes. So far, I have seen no indication of my good students rising to bludgeon Schall to death with their laptops because he would not let them type letters to their friends during class. Ever since Ignatius Reilly referred to him, I have had a special devotion to St. Cassian of Imola, patron of teachers. It is probably worth noting that the "dunces" to whom Jonathan Swift referred were no doubt all of high academic standing.

II.

Actually, the patron saint of professors seems to be the late medieval scholar St. John Cantius. But I did discover a patron saint for "liars and fakes," one for "mediocrity," and one for "handgunners." Even Harry Potter is listed as a patron saint. We academics can piously hope, of course, that a patron saint of teachers or professors is not interchangeable either with one for "liars and fakes" or with one for "mediocrity." The need of an armed professorate sometimes cones up when shootings on campuses occur, as they do with some regularity For the most part we prefer our professors to be "unarmed."

The flip side of this "unarmed professorship" is Machiavelli's "unarmed prophet." The most dangerous people are not necessarily those with guns, but those with odd ideas. Weapons can always be found. Before anyone goes to college or graduate school, he should realize this simple fact: Machiavelli himself was an "unarmed prophet." In that capacity, he was much more dangerous than he ever would have been if, following his own advice, he dressed in armor and rode a charger through the streets of Florence, yelling: "To Arms, To Arms!" He knew that all wars begin first in the mind.

The second semester of any academic year begins after the Christmas holidays. Most universities are not allowed to use that term "Christmas holidays." They still use the term "holiday," even though it really means "holy day." But they may not know that. The theology of it is that you cannot really have a "holiday" if you do not also have a "holy day." Holy days have become mostly recreation days.

At the beginning of a second semester, students who are seniors begin to realize that: "This is it!" They become a bit nostalgic. At the same time, they furiously interview for jobs or apply to law schools. Freshmen are, by now, used to the place. They know where the dining halls are, the library, the classrooms, the ball fields, and probably the local bars. They also have met new friends so that they no longer miss home or high school friends quite as much. They have also taken the measure of many teachers and have heard the opinions of upperclassmen about the rest. In all universities, students have "books" on the professors.

Sophomores and Juniors are probably the best students during this period. They have usually learned to discipline themselves enough to do the work they are expected to accomplish. One of the main impediments to college learning is indeed lack of personal discipline. Even more, it is lack of what used to be called morals. To learn something, we have to be internally free to do so. We need especially to be free from ourselves, from the notion that what "I want" is the most important thing about us. The great adventure of learning begins the day we realize that there is something I really would like to know. I like to add, with Aristotle, that I really would like "to know a thing for its own sake."

One view of college tells us that it is a place to "prepare us for employment." From the time a young student reaches high school, and even worse, college, he is bombarded with the perennial questions: "What do you want to study?" or "What do you want to do with your life to make a living?" Now, I do not disdain such questions. We do need to make a living someday. The whole question of what causes wealth and its distribution is involved here. This is one of the great questions that one ought to confront in life and in college.

The image of the "impractical" professor advising the "impractical" student to plan for an "impractical" life is amusing and common. Student princes, who never want to leave school, are likewise worrisome. Actually, if we read Plato, this suspicion about the nuttiness of academics is generally the common man's view of what goes on in college. It is a place where the sophist is not an unfamiliar figure. "The art of the sophist," Aristotle tells us, "is the semblance of wisdom without the reality, and the sophist is one who makes money from an apparent but unreal wisdom" (165a21–22). Plato said much the same thing of the sophist.

The other, greater, danger in college is ideology. Almost every other talk of Benedict XVI mentioned "relativism." Benedict, when pope, was an academic man and knew of what he spoke. Christopher Derrick once spent a year at Thomas Aquinas College in its early days. He went home to England and wrote a book with the marvelous title: *Escape from Scepticism: Liberal Education as If the Truth Really Mattered*. That title pretty much says it all. I am a great admirer of good titles and of the fine art of escaping from skepticism.

This title is mindful of the remark that Allan Bloom made in his *Closing of the American Mind:* He said that every professor, when entering any classroom in the "best" universities, can assume that all the students before him are already relativists or think they are. Actually, I have found over the years with my students (and I have had many) that they are tempted both by relativism and by truth. They are likely already to know the case for the former, but are surprised and often pleased if a case for the latter can be made, which it can.

This latter enterprise of knowing the truth is why the reading of Aristotle is so important. He is the one that tells us, in the most laconic way possible, that our problem with *what is*, with what is true, is not just a question of knowledge or native intelligence. It begins in the question of how we live, of virtue. We do not avoid this problem by denying a place for virtue itself. Even less can we rely on skepticism, since on its own terms, it might not itself be true.

III.

An editor friend of mine once asked several people to comment on what books they had read the previous year. I never got around to this usually delightful chore. A couple of months later, however, I was in my doctor's office waiting for him to finish with another patient. I was looking at his bookshelves. There I spotted a book by Mark Frost entitled *The Greatest Game Ever Played*. As anyone who knows me will recognize, I think that the understanding of sports is itself one of the great aspects of the philosophic enterprise. A chapter in *Another Sort of Learning* is called precisely: "On the Seriousness of Sports." In any case, when my doctor came in, I told him that I should read this book.

> He said, "Go ahead take it and read it."
> I replied, "I do not like to read anything I do not own."
> He immediately responded, "It's yours."
> This is a real medical man!

This book is about the 1913 U.S. Open Golf Championship. Indeed, it is about the founding of modern golf in Scotland, England, the United States, and throughout the world. I decided to read a passage of the book in class. After the class, one of my students came up and told me that this was one of the greatest books she "had ever read," that she had read it many times. I was rather astounded by this information and promised myself, on that basis alone, that I would finish the book, which I did during Christmas vacation.

Why the book is important "academically" and "humanly," I think, is because it is a splendid example of the discipline and love of something that carries us through to know the excellence of a thing. If we long to know but one excellent thing, we can probably save our souls. The very fact that Francis Quiment, the young American golfer from Brookline, could win the US Open against two great British champions was a drama of riveting magnitude. And a truth is found in golf, as in all sports. It is a game, indeed. It is a skill. But it is a test of the very existence of excellence. The great thing about this book, in retrospect, was that Frost also carried the story through the great early golfers even to their deaths. How these men, who won glory, died is itself part of their story. This too is something that Plato told us about even in the beginning of his *Republic*.

A professor often has occasion to be grateful to his students for pointing him to something that he did not know. In this case, I am not sure whether I would have finished the book that my doctor kindly gave me were it not for a student who had actually read it several times and said to me simply, unexpectedly: "It was the greatest book I ever read." Now since this young lady under my very eyes has now read some Plato, Augustine, and others of that illustrious fame, would she still say that a sports book on the 1913 US Open was so great?

After reading the book, what I would say is that, in many ways, all really great books are the same book. That is, they are searches for the truth, for the excellent, for what we do not have but what we search for. So this intellectual aliveness is what I look for in students. I do not want to know whether they are prepared for law school, but whether they wonder about the truth, especially after they get to law school, where they will probably need it most and find it sparingly. A book of Jay Budziszewski was entitled, *Natural Law for Lawyers*. There is hope, as Benedict XVI said in his great encyclical, *Spe Salvi*.

IV.

Msgr. Robert Sokolowski's book *Phenomenology of the Human Person* often speaks of "the agent of truth." That is, truth is not somehow floating up there somewhere, even though it "exists" before we ourselves know it. It must be known by a knower who can and does know. It exists in a judgment, as Aquinas said. It must be actually known as truth. This central issue, that there is a truth that not only can be known but should be actively known, is what a university is about.

Students return to college each semester from their parental homes. They have a growing realization already that they have already left their father's home, not in the sense that they are not welcome there, but in the sense they have to find their own way in the world. Wendell Berry often points out what a dangerous thing it is for a family today to send a child to college. Jennifer Roback Morse's books, *Love and Economics* and *Smart Sex* are not to be missed. But I mention these sources here to remind us that we belong to a heritage that takes a real family—husband, wife, children—seriously and that understands that intelligence is also what the faith is about.

Second semester in most colleges is basketball season, lacrosse season, baseball season, track season, hockey season, rowing and sailing season. Early in one semester, I ran into a young girl on campus who was in one of my classes. She was on some team—field hockey, I think, or soccer. I asked her how many hours the coach expected of her each day. "Something like three or four." I said to her, with some envy, "I wish professors could demand such hours!"

But let me conclude with this point. Students are not in college to "prepare" for some technique or craft, even the medical or legal professions. In a sense, as Benedict XVI implied in the Regensburg Lecture, they are here for no purpose at all but to know, and know the truth on the grounds alone which truth can be known. On many campuses, there are many outside lectures a day from local, national, and international figures. May I say it? These are distractions, for the most part. Students are not here this time of their lives to find out about current events. And if studying current events is what they do while in the university, that is all they will know. They will have missed the important things while pursuing the ephemeral ones.

Now I am not opposed to "ephemeral" things. This immediacy is largely what my book, *The Sum Total of Human Happiness,* was about. The whole is in the part. But we need time and space to find it. We need conversation and purpose. We need to read, but to read what tells us the truth. We need what Aristotle called *theorein,* contemplation.

But before we can do this, to go back to the "greatest game ever played," we have to find that spark in our soul that knows the relation between what we can and cannot do in this world. We need to put the world in its proper place, and us in it and beyond it. We need to have a taste for the transcendent. We need really to acknowledge that we have restless hearts and souls and why. Undergraduate and most gradates, on leaving school in the springtime, are not really old enough to know fully what goes on within them. Plato, who insisted on this point, was right here.

It is not that we cannot or should not begin to learn something of the highest things in our early years. Like the best golfers, it takes time and experience for most of us even to begin to see the light. Still, and this is what makes university teaching one of the great human adventures, minds become alert before your very eyes. Souls have longings. Nothing less than the truth will satisfy them. This life is not enough, but it is where we all begin because it is where we are.

A student gave me a copy of David Michaelis' *Schulz and Peanuts* for Christmas. As I often do, I find ultimate things in Charlie Brown. On page 192, there is an early cartoon. It shows Schroeder and Charlie sitting on a stoop. Schroeder says, "Guess what I am whistling, Charlie Brown." He then proceeds to whistle something, with the musical notation conveniently given in the cartoon.

After listening, Charlie replies, "'Old Black Joe'? . . . 'Take Me Out to the Ball Game'? . . . 'Home on the Range'?"

Rather annoyed, Schroeder replies to a perplexed Charlie, "Nope, it was the last half of the tenth measure of Sinding's Op. 32, N. 9 . . ."

To this information, Charlie simply says, "Y'know, I almost said that. I don't know why I didn't."

Of course, we all, including Schroeder and Charlie himself, understand that Charlie did not have a clue about what this music was. Nor did I when I read the cartoon. Christian Sinding, it turns out, was a Norwegian composer who died in 1949. I had to look it up myself, as I thought "Sinding" was a misprint. I have never heard his Opus 32, but I am sure my friend Robert Reilly has and will send me a disc of it on request. Reilly's book, *Surprised by Beauty*, is precisely about the glory of much modern music that few of us are aware of.

But this is the point I want to make here. College is to be what it is, a "liberal," that is, "freeing," education. Education means that we seek to know (and see and hear and taste and feel) *what is*. To do this, we must free ourselves. And we free ourselves by encountering the myriads of particular things amid which we live and whose ultimate cause of their being we wonder about.

One ought not to come to college to learn something, unless he comes first to learn everything. That is its real adventure. It is the only real justification for freeing ourselves for four or more years from the busy, un-leisured things that storm about us from every side and for which alone we are told, falsely, that we exist. We cannot, in the end, help but wonder whether Charlie enjoyed the music of Sinding, even if he knew what it was. It is not a sin both to enjoy it and know who wrote it. This is what education is all about.

Saint Cassian of Imola, Pray for Us.

Chapter 2
INTELLECTUAL RESOURCES

The *intellectual resources* you (Brutus) needed were not available at home. So you went to seek them out at Athens, which has always been hailed as the center of scholarship, and you furnished your mind very simply with what they had to offer.
— Cicero, *The Brutus*.[1]

The most wonderful thing is that the best of our convictions cannot be expressed in words. Language is not adequate for everything, and often we are not quite sure whether, in the end, we are seeing, looking, thinking, remembering, fantasizing, or believing.
— Goethe, *The Silence of Goethe*, #63.[2]

I.

We are familiar with the expression "natural resources." Generally, they refer to the myriads of things in the universe that are simply there without any added human intervention. The Epistle to the Hebrews uses the memorable expression "things not made by human hands." This expression would include both finite and infinite things. When we come to think of it, however, man himself is a "natural resource." He is evidently in the world by the same

---

1   Cicero, *"The Brutus: On the Importance of Oratory," On Government*, translated by M. Grant (Harmondsworth: Penguin, 1993), p. 333.
2   Josef Pieper, *The Silence of Goethe*, translated by D. Farrelly (South Bend: St. Augustine's Press, 2009), #63, p. 53.

title as anything else. What-it-is-to-be-man is just there. Man's existence requires no prior human input or intervention. Whenever and wherever he appears, he is already completely *what he is*, though, unlike the rest of material creation, not always as he finally ought to be, which latter also depends on his own freedom, if not grace.

Yet we are now a race that seeks to interfere with ourselves, ostensibly on the grounds that we can do a better job than what caused us to be in the universe in the first place. Our "second" human creation, whereby we decide what we make ourselves to be, will depend on no one other than ourselves. Man himself is also a "given" in the cosmos. But this "givenness" complicates things. Human beings, who are evidently themselves "by nature," can in turn "use" what is there for their own purposes. They can also think about why they are there, something nothing else in the physical cosmos can do.

Generally, this combination of given material things and man's ability to use them has meant to most people that some relation exists between the two. Some animals depend on others for food. Other animals depend on grasses and vegetation. Vegetation depends on water and what is in the soil. Without these dependencies, nothing living would exist. Indeed, the universe was not simply for itself, but for man. It makes no sense if there is no one within it to appreciate it, to know it.

The non-human, physical universe does not think about what it is. It does not declare to itself: "Look, we are dependent on nothing but ourselves!" Probably, we can find no more obvious division of existing things than between those beings that think about things and those which are thought about, granted that the things that think are also thought about. And because we can think about things, evidently, we can use them or relate to them to our own purposes. Most people most of the time have thought that this connection of mind and things simply made sense.

Recent ecological theory has sought to reverse this "primacy of man" relationship. The world, it is claimed, is superior to man. He does not transcend it. Instead of the cosmos being "for man," we now want to instruct ourselves that man is for the cosmos. He is subordinate to it, a mere miniscule part of it. It is greater than he. The "health" of the cosmos subsumes man into itself, not vice versa. Or even more graphically, man is a threat to the cosmos. Evil does not come into the world through man's free will, as was the case in Genesis. It comes because of his very existence in the world and his exigencies.

This "higher" status of the world to man, of course, is itself an idea that does not reside in the cosmos but in some human minds. Ecology and environmentalism as they are explained become a new faith, a new system. It is by no means obvious that the cosmos is more important than the intelligent beings within it. Even more, theories that subordinate man to the cosmos become a new politics of control. Such theories in fact are more political than they are scientific. What the world or universe can "support" is itself subject to theories that purport to know what the capacity of the world is. If man is the real threat to the world, then, obviously, those who control politics in its name will control man. This is why classical totalitarian theory is connected to modern ecological theory.

Since man and his desires are said to be the cause of disorder, they can be reduced to order and enforced by coercion to what our theory allows. Man, in this view, is in the universe. He is to make as little dent on it as possible. He has no transcendent purpose other than keeping the world in steady existence down the ages.

The individual human beings who, at one time or another, inhabit the world have no significance in themselves. Each merely keeps the species alive down the ages. The cosmos is a "success" to the extent that it looks like it did before man appeared, however he appeared. Since, it is said, resources are finite, every generation is responsible for distributing them to every other generation on the basis of what it estimates these resources are. No generation is allowed to use more than its share. Just how this "share" is to be calculated becomes itself a basis of political power.

The mission of this cosmological "over-lordship" of mankind is, supposedly, to keep the earth as it is for those who come later on. It is concerned down the eons, however long that is. Some higher inner-worldly entity, the cosmos itself, becomes what is superior to man. This force is the new "god" (or sometimes "goddess") who rules the ecological world. Now eternity comes to mean not the personal destiny of finite rational persons with God, but the unending cycles of keeping the earth as it was in the beginning. The only trouble with this position is, of course, that the earth, sun, and even the cosmos itself seems to have had a beginning and a given time range. Suns and their planets do burn themselves out.

In any case, man must be restricted, for as long as the earth supports life, so that he does not "deprive" future generations. Thus future generations become more important than present generations. By this logic, we are all now deprived of what we need by the actions of the billions who went before us on this earth, by what they took and did on this earth while they were here. All of this, no doubt, assumes that there have been or will be no discoveries or developments that render the worries of the parsimonious earth out of date. The ecological world is a world without the human mind except as a tool to guarantee no changes in the world.

II.

Cicero used the term "intellectual resources." Obviously, we cannot have such resources before we have intellect and before it acts. Cicero tells us that Brutus went to study in Athens to acquire these resources. Cicero had sent his own son to study in Athens for the same reason, as he tells us in his great treatise *On Duties*. What, we might wonder, is the relation of "intellectual" and "natural" resources? In the time of Cicero, the far north of Europe seems to have been in a primitive state. Why did not Cicero send his son north instead of to Athens? No doubt explorers who went north and later even to the North Pole learned something. But that was because they took with them that power, their minds, by which it is possible to know anything. All the earth was at one point a wasteland, that is, a place on which no human enterprise had taken place.

One of the purposes of the intellect, no doubt, is to articulate what things are. We need to identify them. But we cannot do this identification if we cannot in some sense stand apart from them. We regard them as not being ourselves who are looking at them. They are not us. Yet, in knowledge, they "become" us. To know something is to "become" what that thing is, without our changing it. The world of material things is one thing. The world as known and articulated by intelligent beings is another. Together they remain one world, no doubt, but knowledge by itself, as Aristotle said, changes nothing.

Yet knowledge, once articulated and subject to human will and enterprise, can change things if it knows what they are. Actually, it can change things even if it does not know what they are, but that change will be accidental, not a product of knowing what the change is. The Greeks of Athens distinguished between the theoretical and the practical intellect. By this distinction, they did not mean that we have, as it were, two intellects. Rather, they meant that we have one intellect that can be activated to two different purposes. The first they called "theoretical" intellect. This distinction meant that we could use our minds simply to know what something is. We did not want to do anything with it. We discover a certain delight in simply knowing what things are. In many ways, this desire to know is the deepest drive in us. Man is, by nature, a rational animal. This is his simplest and most profound definition.

The perfection of our mind is really to know what is not ourselves. Socrates talked about "knowing ourselves." But we ourselves are not direct objects of our own knowing powers. What we know and want to know are things not ourselves—*all that is*. Each human mind has this potential capacity to know all that is not itself, including, evidently the causes of things. And even there, we want to know the cause of things as they are in themselves. This seeking to know is what, in its own way, defines us in the highest sense. We are the beings who seek to know all that is not ourselves. We do think that we will not really know ourselves unless we come at ourselves through what is not ourselves. This is why the best definition of truth is simply the conformity of mind and reality.

Practical intellect, on the other hand, art and prudence, brings up another side of our mind. By knowing what things are, by knowing that are not ourselves, we can order them, use them for some purpose of our own. We have the impression that things *that are*, while beautiful, can be made more beautiful. We can find examples of this in buildings, in gardens, in paintings, and in music.

We do not think that it is somehow contrary to what things are to make them more beautiful. We can say, no doubt, that a cathedral does not know that it is beautiful. Maybe the stones protest being in place? We hear complaints that the soil under the freeways and roads of this world protests its subjection to man. But again we ask, just who is doing this protesting? The only answer is not the stone or the soil but human beings imbued with a certain theory that wants to leave the stones in the ground and the roads unpaved.

III.

"The most wonderful thing," Goethe wrote, "is that the best of our convictions cannot be expressed in words." This sentence reflects Plato's famous statement in his Seventh Letter that he has never expressed what he really holds in his written words. Our "intellectual resources," however, include what men have written and spoken—yes, have sung and prophesized. Part of our "intellectual resources" is contained in the fact that nothing we encounter or know is such that we can exhaust it. This inexhaustibility in things comes from the fact that nothing explains itself yet it exists. On one side of its being, it thus goes back to its own origin, which is not itself. No finite being caused itself to come to be. Its explanation depends on the origin of being, in which it participates but which it does not invent.

If we think about this fact that the objects of our very knowing are themselves revelatory of what is more than themselves, we begin to realize the scope of our "intellectual resources." We are in principle not confined to ourselves. Nor do we want to be. We are beings who want to be related to all that is not ourselves. If we look at this fact about ourselves, we come to realized not only are we related to *all things that are* but we are related to those beings which are likewise related to *all that is*.

}23{

In other words, our "intellectual resources" include not only real and existing things, but reflections and thoughts about these things which others of our kind have also pondered and sought to make something of in words and song. These two things about us—that we know existing things and that we know others of our kind open to the same reality—enable us to be joined together through our speech in a common community of *what is*.

Are we, to use Goethe's words, "seeing, looking, thinking, remembering, fantasizing, or believing"? We can, on reflection, distinguish what we are doing. We can see, look, think, remember, fantasize, or believe. But in each case, we have to see something, look at something, think about something, remember something, fantasize about something, or believe about something. These acts are properly ours only if we first know what they are and what they tell us about knowing some existing thing. Our "intellectual resources" are enormous, so enormous that the amount of lifetime we are given is never sufficient so that we might fully know even what we have encountered in our short years in this cosmos.

"Language," as Goethe said, "is not adequate for everything." This inadequacy is because language is the instrument we have as part of our being that enables us to talk about the *things that are*. We do not have language for the sake of language. We have language to take us to the *things that are*. Once we arrive there, we will know that they are in turn themselves inexhaustible, yet also meant for us that we should know them, speak about them to those of our kind whom we know.

No existing thing is complete until someone knows it. This knowing is true even within the Godhead. I suspect, this relationship is why the *Logos* is the *Logos* or Word of the Father. The Father and the *Logos* lead in turn the Spirit out of Whose mission all things come to us. They are gifts that reflect not themselves but that uncreated source in which they were first "seen." What is not God is not God. This fact constitutes its dignity. God remains God while what is not God remains *what it is*.

The "intellectual resources" of the beings that are not God include this understanding of themselves that they are finite. They are indeed not God. We are open to receive what is not ourselves. We can be taught. This conclusion, I think, is what Goethe meant when he said: "Often we are not quite sure whether, in the end, we are seeing, looking, thinking, remembering, fantasizing, or believing." What we are sure of is that we are doing one or the other of these things in our effort to know *what is*. Here is the final source of all both "natural and intellectual resources."

Chapter 3
ON TEACHING[*]

For do teachers profess that it is their thoughts which are perceived and grasped by the students, and not the sciences themselves which they convey through speaking? For who is so stupidly curious as to send his son to school in order that he may learn what the teacher thinks?
— Augustine, *De Magistro*, C. XIV.[1]

The scandalmongers of the secretariat fulfilled a useful purpose—they kept alive the idea that no one was to be trusted. That was better than complacence. Why, he wondered, swerving the car to avoid a dead pye-dog, do I love this place [colonial West Africa] so much? Is it because here human nature hasn't had time to disguise itself? Nobody here could ever talk about a heaven on earth. Heaven remained rigidly in its proper place, on the other side of death, and on this side flourished the injustices, the cruelties, the meanness, that elsewhere people so cleverly hushed up. Here you could love human beings nearly as God loved them, knowing the worst: you didn't love a pose, a pretty dress, a sentiment artfully assumed.
— Graham Greene, *Heart of the Matter*, 1948.[2]

---

[*]   A Lecture given the Faculty at Ave Maria University in Ave Maria, Florida, August 17, 2007. Published in *Vital Speeches*, LXXIII (October 2007), pp. 458–61.

1   St. Augustine, "Concerning the Teacher," *Basic Works*, edited Whitney Oates (New York: Random House, 1948), vol. I, p. 394.

2   Graham Greene, *Heart of the Matter* (Harmondsworth: Penguin, 1971), pp. 35–36.

I.

What does it mean "to teach"? Teaching is correlative to learning. In the end, the successful teacher and the successful pupil know the same truth, which neither of them owns and to which both are subservient. They inhabit the same world, outside of which there can only be strife. I once wrote an essay entitled, "On the Mystery of Teachers I Have Never Met."[3] The best teachers may not be alive when we are. We may teach those who do not yet exist, or those who do exist but whom we shall never meet.

Yet teaching depends on presence. Books make present him who is long dead, who is far away, who speaks a language not our own, yet who is human as we are. I suppose movies, tapes, pictures, discs, and internet do much the same. Truth, to repeat, is not "owned" by anyone. This intrinsic non-ownership is why teachers and learners can have a common good; why they are not, in principle, enemies to each other struggling over disputed possessions. We are not diminished when someone else learns what is true, even with our assistance.

Teachers bring us to the point where we can ourselves see what is at stake. This universality of the cause of truth is occasion for gratitude. To be a teacher means to be grateful that there are those willing to follow us, even correct us, in the pursuit of that to which all of us are subordinate. To be a student means that others can guide us to know what we do not yet know. They do not teach us "their" truth, but bring all of us to the same truth, by which alone we are free.

Augustine bluntly tells us, in his famous tractate on the teacher, that we would be stupid to send our sons to college merely to learn what the teacher himself "thinks." Who cares, really, what the professor "thinks?" But is not the acquiring of such academic knowledge what "research" (that magic word) or scholarship is all about? Do we not seek to find out what teachers "think" in the very act of matriculation? Professors are supposed to "think," after all. Why else do they exist? Thinking itself is a perfection of our nature. The

---

3   Found in James V. Schall, *On the Unseriousness of Human Affairs* (Wilmington: ISI Books, 2001), chapter 5.

ultimate justification of a university is that it is a protected space that has no other purpose but thought and its reachings toward truth.

As students, however, we do not want to have a teacher who never tells us what he "really" thinks about a given issue, especially about great issues. Nothing is more frustrating to a student than to spend hours and semesters with a professor and, in the end, still be "clueless" about what the man thinks. He does not want to "impose" his ideas on the hapless student. This unwillingness to take a stand is perhaps the greatest excuse ever invented for not thinking. The professor spends his hours telling us what Hegel, or Mohammed, or Einstein, or Heidegger "thought." All of this knowledge may be very nice, of course. Is the professor's task merely to outline for us what someone else "holds"? Are there no professors who take us to the truth of things? Are they found in existing universities? Do academic institutions have a monopoly on truth even when they deny that there is truth?

For such a teacher who tells us only what someone else holds, teaching is something like a gas station attendant, when such services still existed. He just puts whatever fuel, regular or supreme, we request into the tank of our automobile. What the attendant himself thinks about the nature of "fuels" is irrelevant except for his ability to distinguish one tank from another. We do not want him to put diesel fuel in our normal gas tank even if we request it. On this model, the effective teacher tells us what someone else holds. No doubt learning what someone else maintains is a worthy endeavor, even if what is learned is wrong. It is impossible to know what we hold without knowing what others hold, of course. The "teaching" comes after this preliminary explication has been accomplished. The end of teaching is that the professor and the student know the same truth, the same reality that neither of them invented, the same procedure by which each arrives at it.

II.

Many universities today pride themselves on the teaching "great books" or having "great teachers." Education is said to be learning what the "great teachers" taught in "great books." The list of what is "great" is, no doubt, variable. If I manage to do a semester course in which I read Plato, Aristotle, Augustine, Aquinas, Machiavelli, and Nietzsche, some student will invariably wonder why we left out Seneca, Niels Bohr, Erasmus, Al Gore, or the Buddha. But if we go back to Augustine's central point, we realize that teaching presupposes "something" to be taught. This something is not itself what is exclusively in the mind of the teacher as its original source, even when the teacher genuinely knows what he is talking about.

This objective basis of what is known is why those fathers are "stupid," as Augustine said, to send their sons to hear frothy collegiate opinions that have no claim to a truth that is independent of the mind of a particular professor. And yet, as Aquinas taught us, truth is in the intellect of an agent affirming or denying insofar as that agent is actually knowing *what is*. In this sense, truth is not "outside" the classroom. It is in its very conversation. To use Robert Sokolowski's phrase, the human person is the "agent" of truth precisely to the degree that he is actually knowing it. The aliveness of truth depends on the aliveness of existing beings endowed with minds that actually know.

Leo Strauss, Frederick Wilhelmsen, and others have pointed out that students who are subjected to the rigors of great books' programs often end up as skeptics. They soon find out that the great teachers contradict each other. Students become "bewildered," as Plato said in book seven of the *Republic,* when he spoke of those who are exposed to philosophy too soon. Beginning philosophy too soon is still one of the greatest dangers in modern education, without closing the question of exactly when to begin. Unprepared and immature students cannot see their way out of the contradictions, the seeing of which way out is the main impetus of philosophy itself. This lining up the contradictions is why Aquinas always began talking of what was true by explaining what was not true and why.

In other words, philosophy has a certain priority over the history of philosophy. Strauss said, in a famous phrase, speaking of political philosophy but equally applicable to the whole discipline, that to confuse the history of philosophy for philosophy itself is to substitute the record of "brilliant errors" for the genuine pursuit of truth itself. As Gilson pointed out in his famous study of the "unity" of philosophical experience, the excitement of philosophy also consists in seeing how close to truth the brilliant errors of the great thinkers really are.

This "seeing," I sometimes think, is the real locus of that excitement over what I call "the life of the mind." Likewise, in theology, the knowledge of orthodoxy includes the knowledge of heresies. And, as Aristotle implied, it is not just a mental exercise. The small errors in the beginning do lead to the large errors in the end, first in thought, next in living. History in one sense is nothing less than the record of these "small errors" writ large seen against a philosophy that acknowledges that truth exists.

III.

Robert Dilenschneider spoke of the relation of technology to what we know. He noted, for instance, that "the amount of text messages sent and received every day exceeds the population of the planet Earth."[4] Considering the number of people who do not yet possess computers, this means that each of us who owns one of the contraptions is speaking to others multiple times daily. He estimates "that 1.5 exabytes of unique information will be generated worldwide in one year. That tops what had been generated in the previous 5000 years." Now, of course, Aristotle and Plato lived in the previous 5000 years, as did St. Paul and Aquinas and, shall we say, numerous others. We are by no means assured by these numbers that what such men taught will be surpassed or even equaled.

We thus must wonder about the difference between knowledge, information, and wisdom. We even must wonder about what are books and libraries. Universities are building "information centers," not libraries. Today, it is not unusual to receive term papers

---

4   Robert Dilenschneider, "New Technologies Will Change Our Lives," *Herald Examiner* July, 2007.

in which not a single library book is cited, only on-line sources that can be reached without the student ever leaving his room. On the other hand, to write such a paper, the student can be almost any place on earth besides his room. No doubt, a huge amount of what previously was only found in libraries is now found on-line. What difference does it make, after all, where the book is "stored"?

On-line courses and universities make us wonder if huge physical plants are really necessary. Homeschooling, which is greatly aided by on-line materials, itself arose largely from disaffection with what is taught in schools and their moral atmosphere. Many new public high schools today, as I noticed walking through two of them in California this summer, have physical plants that would make many colleges or country clubs envious. And it is the very challenge and claim of the small college: that it can do what is essential, that is, teach what is important, better than more expensive and elaborate institutions.

Somewhere recently, I ran across a comment of someone, I forget whom, who said that Google is a kind of god. That is, it is like omniscience, all knowing. If you do not know something, it will provide the information. And if it does not have any information now, it soon will have it. Even if we are not actually using Google to find some fact or essay or knowledge or document, we know it is somehow "out there." It is "alive" just waiting for us to log in. And hundreds and millions of folks can tune into the same item at the same time. The consequence of this vast information network is that we can relax. We do not have to memorize books and tales as the classical and medieval authors did in the days of no easily accessible books.

If we want to know, for instance, what the Island of Guam looks like, we can call it up and get all the basic information, maps, statistics, government, hotels. If we want to find where someone lives or what an address is, or how to get there, it is all there. Any spot in the world can be zeroed in on electronic maps. We can travel by staying at home, or so it seems.

Is teaching then learning to look up things on Google or some other search engine? I am the first to admit that when I cannot find how to do or find something on a computer, I have to find someone who can tell me how it works. Here, often, the young, who have used these machines all their short lives, teach the old who recall pencils, typewriters, and even telephones. We talk of "moving" information. We map not just our cities and states, but the universe itself.

We know more or less how large the physical universe is, and how small the microscopic world is. We want to know if anyone is out there but us. We look at the physical universe; it does not look at us. If there is someone out there, we think that he will want to communicate with us via some standard cosmic number or system that is involved in our understanding of the universe. We think it strange that we are alone in the universe even if we do not believe in God—perhaps especially if we do not believe in God.

IV.

What does it mean "to teach"? If finally Google had all the information in the world on-line at our finger-tips in our own rooms, would we be happy? Would we have anything to say to each other? Our conversation would be to sit around and ask each other questions on Google. Even today, Google makes factual disputes less interesting. We do not have to wonder about answers to obscure questions, like batting averages or the largest bass caught in Ohio in 1998. But in knowing such things, would we know what we need to know to be what we are, what is important, to achieve our purpose?

Charlie Brown is on the mound, glove in hand, hat skewered, pulled down over his eyes. Lucy is standing behind him. She asks him: "Charlie Brown, what would you do if you were suddenly called into the army?"

To this question out of nowhere, Charlie yells in reply, "HOW SHOULD I KNOW?"

To which Lucy logically responds, "Well, don't you worry about it?"

As Lucy quietly stands by waiting for his answer, Charlie says, less forcefully, "OF COURSE NOT!"

Finally, gritting his teeth at her response, Charlie hears her ask "How come you never worry about things like that?"[5]

Is there a kind of teaching that worries about important things? Are there things that are not on Google or even in what professors think? Would it be a good idea to have just one course in every subject taught the same way throughout the world on the same channel whereby all students could tune in to the same great teacher teaching the same great book?

If we go back to Augustine's discussion of teaching, he explains what he means about not wanting to send one's sons to hear what a professor thinks. Admittedly, Augustine tells his son, the teachers of science, virtue, and wisdom do use words, the meaning of which the student needs to learn. When the pupil hears the words of the professor, he is to "consider within" himself whether what he has heard is "the truth." Does whatever the pupil thinks become true? Hardly. We are rather to look at the "interior truth" in as much as we can. "Thus they (the pupils) learn and when the interior truth makes known to them that true things have been said, they applaud." What a remarkable passage! It is the last thing we would expect.

That applause, I have always thought, is a marvelous reaction to the teaching experience. It is the true reward of the teacher, even though, as Augustine will tell us, it is not primarily for him. But for a teacher, there is nothing more satisfactory than to see a student suddenly see the truth of something. Most students quickly catch the measure of their teachers, their foibles, prejudices, and even lies. They are not taught by gods who are already wise, but by teachers who also have come to know what they know only gradually.

What is the applause for? Students are not primarily applauding the teacher, Augustine thinks. They are applauding themselves as "learners," but only if "teachers know what they are saying." The teacher always learns anew from teaching what is itself great.

---

5   *The Complete Peanuts*, v. 4, 7-11-1957.

He too applauds the same truth. It is like the great conductor who applauds his orchestra after both complete a great work of music. All are delighted in what now comes to be seen or heard because it is true, because it is there, because it is beautiful

Yet, "men are mistaken." Teachers can be called such "who are not." Christ Himself said, "do not call me teacher," meaning of course that He too is sent to reveal His Father. All teaching, I think, has this emphasis, this background, that it is not ours. We do not ourselves make it what it is. More basically, we do not ourselves make *what is*.

V.

What is it to teach? I return to Lucy's question to Charlie Brown: "How come we never worry about things like that?" The great questions are only questions when they have answers. Why is there something, not nothing? Why do I exist? Why am I not nothing? Why is this thing not that thing? How is it possible to know what I do not cause to be? Many questions are answered, however, as we learn from Google. This leads us to suspect that all questions have answers if we only knew where to find them.

In the beginning, besides Augustine I cited a passage from Graham Green. It was a passage that reflected our abiding inner-worldly imperfections and why it is dangerous to think we can replace them by our own powers. It was somehow a statement of the love of human life even when it is not perfect. "Heaven remained rigidly in its proper place, on the other side of death." No statement is more politically important than this one. This is a statement worthy of Augustine's political realism. The greatest thing the great teachers teach us is that we are not in total charge of the reality we have been given. "Here you could love human beings nearly as God loved them, knowing the worst . . ." This is a great teaching. I for one applaud it.

In a lecture entitled "Political Vision and the Praxis of Politics," Joseph Ratzinger reflected:

Man *qua* man remains the same in primitive conditions as in technologically developed societies and does not advance to a higher level simply by the fact that he has learned to employ more highly developed tools. Human nature starts over from the beginning in every human being. Therefore there cannot be such a thing as a definitely new, advanced, and smooth running society. Not only was this the hope of the grand ideologies, but it has been becoming more and more the general objective expected by all ever since hope in the hereafter was demolished. A definitely well-run society would presuppose the end of freedom.[6]

Greene had said that we must keep the dreams of utopia on the other side of death. Ratzinger tells us, in a remarkable insight, that since the "hope of the hereafter has been demolished," we more and more demand perfection in this world.

Great teachers are those who, in all they do, keep this distinction between this world and the next straight. The universe is created for man. But man is created for a life that he does not himself define, only receives as a gift. It is given to him even though he lives in sin and the valley of tears.

The last words in Augustine's treaties on the teacher are those of Adeodatus, his son, explaining what he has learned

through being reminded by your words that man is only prompted by words in order that he may learn, and it is apparent that only a very small measure of what a speaker thinks is expressed in his words. Moreover, when He (Christ) spoke among the people He reminded us that we learn whether things are true from that one only whose habitation is within us, whom now, by His grace, I shall so love more ardently as I progress in understanding.

6 Joseph Cardinal Ratzinger, "Political Vision and the Praxis of Politics," *Europe: Today and Tomorrow*, (San Francisco: Ignatius Press, 2007), p. 62.

Words prompt us to learn but what is meant is so much richer than our words. Reality is more than our ability to formulate what it is. The "habitation" of ultimate truth is within us. The world of *what is* exists also to be in correspondence with the world that we know within ourselves. What we are taught by the Word, by the great teachers, is not words, but what they mean, and through them, what it is meant by the fact that truth first resides in things where its richness is beyond our words. This is why we applaud, that in knowing what we know, we know that there is so much more. The consolation of the teacher, at its highest, is when he realizes that his students, however grateful, see beyond him to *what is* and to the mystery of why something *is* rather than is not.

Chapter 4
WHY PROFESSORS NEED STUDENTS
AND OTHER PHILOSOPHICAL FABLES*

A teacher in such a (democratic) community is afraid of
his students and flatters them, while the students despise
their teachers or tutors. And, in general, the young imitate their elders and compete with them in word and
deed, while the old stoop to the level of the young and are
full of play and pleasantry, imitating the young for fear of
appearing disagreeable and authoritarian.
— Plato *Republic*, VII, (563a).

For the perplexity of life arises from there being too many
interesting things in it for us to be interested properly in
any of them; what we call its triviality is really the tag-
ends of numberless *tales* . . .
— G. K. Chesterton, "The Secret of a Train."[1]

The majority never read anything twice. The sure mark of
an unliterary man is that he considers "I've read it already"
to be a conclusive argument against reading a work. ...
Those who read great works . . . will read the same work
ten, twenty or thirty times during the course of their life.
— C. S. Lewis, *An Experiment in Criticism*, 1961.[2]

---

*   A Lecture given at the University of North Dakota at Grand Forks, October
     8, 2007. Published in *Vital Speeches*, LXXIV (March 2008), pp. 28–33.
1   G. K. Chesterton, "The Secret of a Train," *Tremendous Trifles* (New York:
     Sheed & Ward, 1955), p. 14.
2   C. S. Lewis, *An Experiment in Criticism* (New York: Macmillan, 1961), p. 2.

I.

The program here at the University of North Dakota is called "People You Should Meet." It is indeed an honor to be included in this select group. The program's title, I note, is not "People You Should Love to Meet." People you perhaps should meet may not be ones whom you would "love" to meet. Likewise, the program's title brings up its converse formulation: Are there "People You Should *Not* Meet," even if you would "love" to meet them?

Would any university, I wonder, sponsor a program entitled, "People You Should *Not* Meet," however interesting or odious they might be? One thinks also of people like Oedipus meeting his father at the crossroads or Iago, the malicious presence in Shakespeare's *Othello*. Yet if we do not meet either Oedipus or Iago in our studies, we are not serious students or fortunate in our teachers. We all, I suspect, could more quickly add to the list of "not-to-be-mets" than to that of "should-meets." Recalling Oedipus and Iago, moreover, discussions of providence concern people, great and small, who encounter those who carry them, for better or worse, to what Tolkien calls their "doom." Every existing human being is the result of a chance meeting, at some point in time, between his actual mother and father.

Yves Simon observes soberly that "nothing protects the young philosopher against the risk of delivering his soul to error by choosing his teachers infelicitously."[3] This remark is delicately put. It alerts us to the perplexing depths of the professor-student relationship. It reminds us that not everyone with rank and tenure, on that score alone, is necessarily someone on whom we can rely. Many of the Kentucky novelist Wendell Berry's stories are based on the dire effects on good families of simply sending their offspring off to college.

Nor, for their part, are all students readily willing to do the work necessary to learn something by seeing reasons for it.

---

3   Yves Simon, *A General Theory of Authority* (Notre Dame: University of Notre Dame Press, 1980), p. 100.

Aristotle was eloquent about the relation, even from childhood, of good habits to the willingness to learn what is true. In Simon's dictum, the emphasis is on the "to whom" the young scholar "delivers his soul." Obviously a relationship exists between what we learn and the integrity of those who teach us. Simon presupposes that we are dealing with free souls. They give themselves freely, if perhaps uncritically, to unworthy teachers. This freedom pertains both to the student and to the teacher. Freedom of will is part of what it means to be a human being even in his knowing. It is our use of will, after all, that guides us to the arguments we choose to employ in explaining and justifying our actions.

What, then, is the essence of the student-professor relationship? The "professor" has a particular status by his very title. Students hear of something called "rank and tenure." "Rank and tenure," aside from settling relationships of professors with academic and civil administrators, implies "authority," as Simon put it. It means that a professor is "qualified" by someone other than himself to teach. The professor is not just anyone off the streets.

A professor must, as they say, prove himself before his "peers," who also can have their limitations and prejudices. We have no trouble understanding this criterion when we think of our doctor or lawyer. Each is to prove his "qualification" to exercise a certain function. We need reasons to trust those who deal in our affairs. Robert Sokolowski discusses this relationship in his essay, "The Fiduciary Relationship and the Nature of the Professions."[4] None of us goes willingly to what is known as a "quack."

The same point is made by recalling that, strictly speaking, a professor is not paid a salary or wages. He is not being remunerated for his "labor" in terms of dollars per hour. Nor are students "paying" him for his "work." A professor's income is called an "honorarium." Honor is a sign of something higher than justice. We are not "buying" anything from professors. Academia is not, as such, a market, however valuable markets may be. What a professor

---

4   Robert Sokolowski, *Christian Faith & Human Understanding* (Washington: Catholic University of America Press, 2006), pp. 250–67.

knows and has is given freely to students with no other return than what, "for its own sake," is known and true for everyone.

We recognize that professors must stay alive with considerable leisure. Honoraria have no other purpose but to allow professors to pursue some idea or work wherever it goes. Nor is what we receive from a professor ours as if we have some proprietary claim to it. What is true in principle belongs to everyone on the same terms, on the willingness and discipline that it takes to learn that *what is* exists as it is.

The notion of academic "rank," moreover, is related not only to knowledge but to wisdom. Those who know more, who are more "sagacious," are "ranked" higher. This ranking grounds the distinctions between professors themselves—assistant, associate, full. Rank implies that the professor knows more than his own narrow field, though he is to know that also if he has one. He begins at last to see how it all fits together. As Aquinas said, *sapientis est ordinare*; it is the function of the wise man to order things.

Relative "rank" reflects the old medieval guild idea that someone becomes more and more proficient in a craft by proving gradually over time that he knows how to incorporate its best standards. A "master-piece" indicated a craftsman's ability to produce what is excellent in his trade. In the academy, the "master-piece" is the defense of a thesis. In the area of thought, truth is elaborated and passed on to new generations of students. The masterpiece does not exclusively have to do with the publication of books, though that is surely one of its signs. But again, to return to Simon, a professor can enchant us or deflect our souls from *what is*.

II.

What after all is a professor? Or, even more profoundly, what is the relation of student and professor? Why do they belong to the same world? This world is usually called, after Plato, the "academy." The academy, when politically allowed to exist, which is not everywhere the case, is an institution that stands outside of state, church, economy, family, and popular opinion. Historically, the university was set up, usually by the Church or a prince, to encourage conditions for acquiring knowledge "for its own sake" to occur. The university—*universitas*, i. e. all disciplines—arose out of medieval perplexities over claims of reason and revelation, over a system of posing questions so that answers could systematically be given in a way that could be understood and handed on to subsequent students.

We begin our search for knowledge with perplexities. We do not want to end there. In a sequence that sharp students will understand is filled with metaphysics and epistemology, Lucy is showing an enthusiastic Charlie Brown a gift that she has received.

"Look!" she says, "My dad bought me a stuffed dog!"

To this news, Charlie replies, "Gee! Is it a real stuffed Dog, Lucy?"

Looking down at the gift, Lucy, with some consternation, replies, "Of course, it's a real stuffed dog! No, I mean it isn't a real dog because it's stuffed and it's . . . well . . . I mean . . ."

Charlie just looks on with evident curiosity. Lucy continues, almost crying, "What I mean is that it's stuffed and it's real but yet it . . . well . . . I mean . . . I . . . I . . ." Charlie continues to stare at her unaccustomed uncertainty.

Finally, Lucy becomes furious. With evident intellectual frustration she yells at Charlie, "WHY DO YOU ASK ME SUCH THINGS?"[5]

The university is a place where "such things" can hopefully be asked, but only if we have a philosophy that acknowledges that questions have or can have intelligible answers. If our philosophic presuppositions, in effect, allow no answers to any questions, we cannot have a university, only a debating society that allows no verdict. The reality of the "real" stuffed dog and its relation to a "real" dog is, after all, a metaphysical question, as is the question of what we know when we know as real both a dog and a stuffed

5   *The Complete Peanuts*, 1955–956 (Seattle: Fantagraphics Books, 2004), 4-22-1956, p. 271.

dog. The epistemological question is: how is it that we know and know that we know, whatever it is that we know, a dog or a stuffed dog?

Many brilliant men and women, of course, are not formally professors. We know that people with sanity and common sense can teach us much that we need to know about how to live. This practical learning is one of the reasons we have parents and grand-parents. Most of us will spend most of our lives *not* in a university. The world and the knowledge of the world are not the same things. The reality of a university, after all, is that students, in a few short years, leave it. It would be "unnatural" if they did not. We are not to be "student princes" all of our lives. Life is larger than the university, something most undergraduate students already suspect. The lives of their professors give them added proof, if they need it.

Certainly, we can learn something from almost anyone. But the professor-student relationship is not simply the learning of anything from just somebody. The university seeks truth, but it is not its sole custodian and sometimes not its best. On leaving the hapless professors behind to age at their own speed, year after year students leave the university to pursue their own lives. Hopefully, they do not suddenly cease their quest, their wonder about what it all means.

The whole point of a university is that students freely continue in their own way what was merely begun when they first reached adulthood. A. D. Sertillanges' famous book, *The Intellectual Life,* was designed precisely to facilitate this continuation.[6] In the seventh book of the *Republic*, Plato carefully points out that the best learning only begins long after we have graduated from college. Most professors know this from their own experience.

But professors, like all students, needed a beginning. Both professors and students need something that can only be called inspiration or light to incite them to a pursuit that takes all their lives and probably more, if the end of the *Republic* is to be believed. As C. S. Lewis intimated, we have not read a great book at all if we

---

6   A. D. Sertillanges, *The Intellectual Life* (Washington: The Catholic University of America Press, [1921] 1998).

only have read it once. To this admirable insight, my addendum is simply that a professor exists to facilitate the first reading of his students without which a second one is not metaphysically possible or, often, humanly speaking, likely.

In the passage from the *Republic* that I cited in the beginning, Socrates describes a democracy wherein unrestricted "liberty" is the principle of order. Here he notices the absurdity of professors who try to be like their students, who imitate the manners and dress of Joe College, who part their hair the same way, if they have any left to part. What is behind Plato's concern here is that professors with this sophomoric mentality have little to teach their students.

Nor, to pass to Aristotle, is the professor-student relation, as such, one of personal friendship. Friendship is indeed that to which the pursuit of truth and goodness directs us. But that is beyond the academy, though it is not beyond the students and their relation to each other. Students are invariably amazed when they read what Aristotle says about friendship, what it is, its different kinds, how it comes about, how it is lost. Professors and students, none the less, are not "pals."

The relationship of professor to student, for the good of both, is formal, though hopefully friendly and of mutual good will. The temptation of professors is to be song and dance men, that is, entertainers.[7] And they should not lack humor. Still, over a life time, a professor will be lucky to acquire a few good friends from among those he has taught now grown. Indeed, Aristotle says we will be fortunate to have a few friends of the highest sort at all in the course of a lifetime. This truth is one of the greatest perplexities in all of moral philosophy, one that ultimately, as Aristotle intimated, reaches the Godhead itself.[8]

---

7 See James V. Schall, "What a Student Owes His Teacher," *Another Sort of Learning* (San Francisco: Ignatius Press, 1988), pp. 32–37.

8 See James V. Schall, "Friendship and Political Philosophy," *At the Limits of Political Philosophy: From 'Brilliant Errors' to Things of Uncommon Importance* (Washington: The Catholic University of America Press, 1996), 218–37; "Unknown to the Ancients: God and Friendship," *What Is God Like?* (Collegeville, MN.: Michael Glazer, 1992), pp. 140–70.

But in teaching, standards and distinctions between student performance and intelligence have to be established. This difference already implies a certain distance between student and teacher, one maintained for the good of both. In other words, it is not unfriendly to give a C- student a C-. It is unjust to do otherwise. But ultimately nothing prevents C- students from becoming good human beings and eventually, by persistent effort, learning more about life than their "higher-IQed" companions.

Though not its essence, an element of justice is found in all teaching in so far as standards exist and must be met. With no standards, no university is possible. Standards are not simply made up by the professors. They do not change from school to school or from time to time, except in their own order from the constant use of reason. Yet, in spite all of this talk of standards, a student at his best simply desires to learn what he can, however little or much it is. He seeks to do so no matter what his IQ. It is a dull professor who does not often notice that those who are interested in learning what he has to say are not always those with the highest qualifications.

The relation of professor to student is, as I like to say, essentially "spiritual." The word "spiritual" does not mean "fuzzy." What does it mean? That professor and student talk of their pious or moral life? No, such exchanges, certainly valid in themselves, belong somewhere else, with parents, counselors, priests, and, yes, friends. Concern for inner moral life of students is not the specific rubric under which a professor as professor deals with them. A "spiritual" relation between student and professor rather refers to what goes on between them in terms of the formality in which they are related. The constant reading of Plato, which, in my view, is necessary for a university to be a university, should make us ever aware that what we both discover is already there.

The first principle, as we have seen, is that knowledge is not "owned" by the professor, the student, the university, or the state. It is not a thing that can be cut up and claimed. It is free and freeing, which is the central meaning of a "liberal" education. That is, it deals with those things that are universally free, universally open to all of us because they are true. They are there to be found whether we find them or not. They are known "for their own sake," as Aristotle said. The old witticism stated that "education" is what happens when the notes of the professor are copied into the notebooks (or now computers) of the student but pass through the minds of neither. What counts, however, is what does pass through the minds of both. This "passing" is what goes on in a university at its best.

A great professor is humble enough to realize that he does not "make" but discovers a truth that itself has a basis in *what is,* in being, in reality. A student's course may not end for years after the last tests are completed if he is still pondering, remembering, and re-reading what he had once read and considered. What the student comes to know by following the guidance of a wise professor is simply the truth of something, of a hint at all things. Neither student nor professor "owns" it. Both understand by the workings of minds oriented to the same reality. Neither professor nor student gave himself what it is to be a being endowed with a mind. Our minds are measured by *what is,* not by their own makings or constructs, except, as Aristotle says, in art—*recta ratio factabilium.*

In the beginning, I cited C. S. Lewis about reading the same book many times in one's life and always learning something new from it. I assure you this is what does happen. One of the inestimable privileges of an aging, if not aged, professor is precisely the opportunity to read and re-read the same book with ever changing students' faces before him. In Aristotle's sense, this experience provides almost the only really leisured life in our society. Every time I re-read a book of Plato, Aristotle, Augustine, or Aquinas, I shake my head and wonder why I had not seen that before. The answer is most likely that I was not yet ready to see it. We do not see all things when we are young, which is why I have all my students read Cicero's *De Senectute*; for they should know something of old age before it happens to them.

III.

In this context, we also recall Plato's concern with the sophists, with those teachers who are only in the business for money or for adulation or prestige. They are the academic version of the Pharisees in the New Testament. Plato, indeed, was devastating in his critique of the sophists. A principal theme of Platonic dialogues was why the philosopher was not accepted in the city. It was, Plato thought, because the city had a disorder of soul that it did not want to face or correct. In the *Sophist*, we read:

> Certainly the genuine philosophers who "haunt our cities"—by contrast to the fake ones—take on all sorts of different appearances just because of other people's ignorance. As philosophers look down from above at the lives of those below them, some people think they're worthless and others think they're worth everything in the world. Sometimes they take on the appearance of statesmen, and sometimes of sophists. Sometimes, too, they might give the impression that they're completely insane (216c–d).

For Plato, in a society that acknowledges no distinction of excellence, of right and wrong, the wise man would appear to most to be mad or a fool. All of education depends on understanding what Plato means when he says that the "genuine" philosopher "haunts" the city. To keep this "haunting" alive is why we have professors and why we have students who wonder about it.

I encourage students to "haunt" used book stores. I do not recommend used computer stores. Last spring, a student from the previous year gave me a battered 1914 Oxford University Press edition of *A Book of English Essays*, which was volume CLXXII of the World's Classics. The inscription was dated "Candlemas, 2007." In the book were essays of Hazlitt, Swift, Dryden, Samuel Johnson—my favorite—among others.

A sentence from the essay of George Eliot entitled simply "Authorship" struck me. "It is for art to present images of a lovelier order than the actual, gently winning the affections, and so determining the taste."[9] This sentence is but another way of putting Plato's city in speech, of the need to know what is just even if we be not just. This passage recalls also the conclusion of the last book of Lewis' *Chronicles of Narnia*, where it said that, after all, it is all "in Plato."[10]

If one comes from a background of political philosophy, as I do, he is aware of the potential disruptive force of "images of a lovelier order." Such images have both Platonic and Christian origins. Who can forget that Plato's book on the *Republic* has, with appropriate nuances, the same title as Augustine's book *De Civitate Dei*? Both understand actual cities, both understand cities in speech and transcendent cities. Both know that our kind cannot be sane without both existing and transcendent cities. This too is what professors have to teach students who are the first to wonder about the origins and destiny of the unsettling reality in which they find themselves already enmeshed.

In the 2006 "Regensburg Lecture," Benedict XVI cited the following passage from Plato's *Phaedo*, the dialogue on the death of Socrates after his Trial in Athens, where, as I like to put it, the "best existing city killed the best man."[11] This passage is pertinent to our topic of professors and students. Indeed, the first part of the "Regensburg Lecture" contained a description of what a university is.[12] Benedict, former German professor that he is, was quick to see the pertinence of Plato's insight for his Regensburg audience, which consisted largely of professors and students.

The young men in the dialogue, not unlike the experience of most college students, became restless over the many confusing,

---

9   George Eliot, "Authorship," *A Book of English Essays 1600–1900* (London: Humphrey Milford/Oxford University Press, 1914), p. 323.

10 See James V. Schall, "The Beginning of the Real Story," *Revisiting Narnia: Fantasy, Myth, and Religion in C. S. Lewis' Chronicles* (Dallas: Benbella Books, 2005), pp. 147–59.

11 See James V. Schall, "The Death of Plato," *The American Scholar*, 65 (Summer 1996), pp. 401–15.

12 The text is found in James V. Schall, *The Regensburg Lecture* (South Bend, IN.: St. Augustine's Press, 2007), Appendix I. Chapter I, "A University Lecture," 18-40. The citation from the *Phaedo* is found in #61, p. 146.

contradictory, and false opinions heard among the learned. They too did not want foolishly to give their souls over to unworthy professors. The youth were discouraged and tempted to give up. To this situation, Socrates responds: "It would be easily understandable if someone became so annoyed at all these false notions that for the rest of his life he despised and mocked all talk about being—but in this way he would be deprived of the truth of existence and would suffer a great loss" (90c-d). This is a marvelous passage. Socrates knows the temptation to wash one's hands of academic confusions. But he also does not want us to be, as he put it, "deprived of the truth of existence." He knows the great loss that would follow in our souls.

IV.

In conclusion, let me return to the passage from Chesterton cited in the beginning. In his essay on "The Secret of a Train," Chesterton is at an English railroad station between Oxford and Paddington. Here he encountered a tale that he did not know except its ending in death. With this experience, Chesterton came to the same "perplexity of life" that we have encountered all along in our discussion of professors and students. He touched on a point that we referred to in Aristotle's discussion of friendship. There Aristotle was aware that we do not have enough time in one lifetime to be friends with everyone.[13]

To have the best in this life, we cannot have everything at once. We must wait for things to unfold. We must choose rightly when they do. Many things appear "trivial" to us, but this is often only because we do not see the whole story. We do not see how they are vital to other lives. In one sense, as I believe Jane Austen implied in *Northanger Abbey*, novelists exist to tell us of lives that we ourselves do not and could not live. The fact that we have minds that can read or hear tales means that we can "live," as it were, more

---

13 See James V. Schall, "Aristotle on Friendship," *The Classical Bulletin*, 65 (#3–4, 1989), 83–88,

lives than our own. Professors exist in part to lead students to lives neither of them will ever know except in speech, as Plato said, or in grace, as Augustine said.

Literary knowledge of other lives does not mean that we do not live our own unique lives with their own unrepeatable dramas of chance and choice. "Too many interesting things" are indeed in other lives for us to be "interested properly in any of them" but our own. The other "philosophic fables," the "numberless tales," as Chesterton called them, are also for us to know. This is why professors need students. They need to have someone to whom to tell fables and tales. Aristotle was right; these things are "for their own sake." "It is for art to present the images of a lovelier order than the actual." "It would be understandable if someone became so annoyed at all these false notions that for the rest of his life he despised and mocked all talk of being."

Yet, it would be a pity if this annoyance led us to bitterness. We would suffer a great loss if we were to be "deprived of the truth of existence." The great teacher Plato warned us about this deprivation. Millennia later, the professor Pope also recalled it to our attention: "The perplexity of life arises from there being too many interesting things in it for us to be properly interested in any one of them."

But we would not, professors or students, want it otherwise. Our minds are open to *all that is*. They are *capax omnium*, able to hold all things. The adventure on which we ourselves are embarked, because of the fact that we live at all, does not exclude the tales of others, the hearing of which, for the thirtieth time, as Tolkien and Lewis taught us, is part of our being, perhaps its perfection. Such are the things to which professors guide students, to the wonder that anything at all exists and is, as students discover, abidingly fascinating.

Chapter 5
QUESTIONS PROPER TO THE UNIVERSITY*

The study of virtue and vice must be accompanied by an inquiry into what is false and true of existence in general and must be carried on by constant practices throughout a long period . . . . Hardly after practicing detailed comparisons of names and definitions and visual and other sense perceptions, after scrutinizing them in benevolent disputation by the use of question and answer without jealousy, at last in a flash understanding of each blazes up, and the mind, as it exerts all its powers to the limit of human capacity, is flooded with light."
— Plato, *The Seventh Letter*, 344b.

The challenges have to do with the truth about man in his personal and social dimension; about the world with its laws which have to be discovered and put to use for the good of humanity; and the *truth about God* the foundation of being, to whom all is to lead and who *alone* gives ultimate meaning to man and to the world. These are *questions which are proper to the university* . . .
— John Paul II, "On the Catholic Universities," 1989.[1]

---

* A Lecture Given at the Convention of the Cardinal Newman Society, Washington, DC, November 8, 2003.

1 John Paul II, "On the Catholic Universities," Address to the Third International Meeting of Catholic Universities and Institutions of Higher Learning, April 25, 1989, in *The Pope Speaks*, 34 (#3, 1989), p. 263.

I.

In his famous *Seventh Letter*, Plato said that the study of virtue and vice was to be pursued into the question of existence itself, into what is true and false. It even implied that, in some basic sense, we will not solve the issues of existence until we first have it right about virtue and vice. This inquiry, moreover, takes much time. We are to ask questions and propose answers. We are to be honest; no jealousy is to prevent us from seeing what is there. Our disputation is to be "benevolent." Finally, if we persist, a "flash understanding" blazes up, consequent to our honest inquiry. Our mind is extended to its limits. We are flooded by light.

Clearly, Plato is describing something that can, and, hopefully, should happen to us if, and perhaps only if, we follow his method and if we possess that *eros* for the truth that best describes the Platonic quest. I say "perhaps" if we follow these slower methods, because Plato himself is also the author of the *Phaedrus* in which he says that, in the experiences of catharsis, suffering, poetry, and love, reality can come to us of a sudden by-passing these slow and careful ruminations that properly belong to the philosophic methods. Aristotle too had implied that ordinary people, if they be good and observant, could arrive at philosophic truths and insights by intuition and insight that did not necessarily presuppose philosophic method.

If, then, we should inquire: "Why does a gas (petrol) station exist?" we would say that it exists for the refueling and repairing of automobiles. Notice, we take for granted that we already know both that and why there are automobiles. Moreover, if it comes up, we could answer this latter question of "Why automobiles?" by explaining the existence of automobiles in terms of certain specific automotive and scientific inventions that have occurred over the past century or so. Presumably, the answer to the question, "Why automobiles in the first place?" would need also a "purpose" answer, a final cause answer. We wanted, as in the case of ships, planes, railroads, and bicycles, a much quicker and less burdensome way to move ourselves and our goods around the neighborhood and the world. Things like snow-mobiles and dune-buggies would probably require another consideration under the heading of pleasure, not just need.

We would also like to do this moving about our towns and country-sides in safety. No doubt, there is a certain danger in automobile driving and riding. In addition to gas stations, we have "engine and body shops" to attend to wrecked cars. I read recently that each day in the United States there are killed in auto accidents the equivalent of a fully loaded passenger plane. Some two and a half million accidents of one sort or another occur every year. Presumably, analogous numbers are found in other countries' statistics. But I suppose we could also argue that, without the automobile, many more would die in other ways, so, on the whole, we can live with the down-side of the existence of Fords, Mercedes, and Toyotas. Before there were autos, all people still eventually died. These machines, together with their truck counterparts, make it possible for huge populations to spread out and for many people to live in relative convenience and comfort. The whole world is rushing to catch up.

II.

But suppose we ask the question: "Why do universities exist?" We find a rather more perplexing problem. We don't "need" universities in the same way we "need" automobiles. We may need them more, but, like all good things, if they go wrong, we may find them dangerous. We belong to a tradition, in fact, that suggests that the nearer a thing is to spirit, the more capable it is of goodness, the more dangerous it is if it goes wrong. The figure of Lucifer stands as an abiding reminder of this principle, one valid not merely for the angelic orders. We are wont to maintain that we "need" universities more than we need automobiles. But the product of universities is rather less visible and tangible than the product of General Motors. And when universities go wrong, their damage far surpasses the frightful figures of automobile deaths and accidents.

John Paul II stated frankly that nations and cultures need universities, need them to be what they are. He implied that a distinct nature or rationale is to be found for what-is-it-to-be a university. The Church likewise, he thought, needs universities. Indeed, universities as we know them arose "from the heart of the Church" historically. "You must always keep in mind that it is *not only the Church* which stands in need of them (universities)," John Paul II, speaking specifically of Catholic universities, observed in 1989, but also "*Society too, throughout the world, looks to these universities and needs them . . . because there is a great deal that the world can receive from Catholic universities.*"[2] The Church is not the academy; the academy is not the polity, the polity is neither the academy nor the Church. When any of these institutions claims the function of the other, we rightly call it totalitarian.

Behind universities, as we know them, of course, we find in our history the Academy of Plato, the Lycaeum of Aristotle, the Porch of the Stoics, Cicero's orations, the works of Augustine and the Church Fathers, as well as the monasteries of St. Benedict and the Cathedral Schools of the Middle Ages. Oxford, Cambridge, Paris, the Italian schools, even the Jesuits, come out of this tradition. The so-called "modern" university with its wide variety of speculative and practical faculties itself recalls the German academic tradition and much American adaptation to all of these traditions.

In this light, however, I have often been impressed with a remark of Eric Voegelin with regard to the founding of the Platonic Academy, that famous institution that lasted into the Byzantine times of Justinian. It still forms much of our intellectual heritage. I repeat this observation here because I think it pertinent to our present problems. Voegelin understood the Athenian tradition to be one of an actual civic pursuit of truth and beauty in the theaters, dramas, public works, and arts of the City. The City, that is to say, its citizens in their attendance, had actively witnessed the tragedies and comedies of its great poets. They experienced there a profound wonderment about life and death depicted in the Greek theater.

2   Ibid., pp. 261–62.

When, however, the philosopher Socrates was killed by the city of Athens, philosophy, Voegelin thought, fled to the academy. Truth was not safe in the city. The actual Athenians did not recognize the ultimate issues when they were played out in their own city's life, before their very eyes. Suddenly, it was no longer in the city where the highest questions could be asked and pondered, but only apart from it, in a place protected from the disorder of souls revealed in a city that would kill its best man. It was only in the "academy" where the fundamental questions of man could be asked.

And it was dangerous business to ask them, even in the academy. The academy could ponder the truth of things precisely because it could quietly read and reread the dialogues of Plato or the lectures of Aristotle. They were dangerous books. If our souls were not rightly ordered in the city, through the habitual learning of virtues and rejection of vices, we had a chance to accomplish this discipline and pursuit in the academy.

III.

In this regard, I am fond of citing the reflections of the German-English economist E. F. Schumacher. In his *A Guide for the Perplexed*, a book itself with medieval overtones, he tells us of his first going to Oxford after World War II, then perhaps the premier university in the world. When, as a young man, he arrived there, he discovered that none of the things most important to our souls was being taught or even mentioned. The methods taught made it impossible even to ask the most fundamental questions. He understood there was a reason for this neglect, a reason that had something to do with the history of modern thought, a history which he proceeded to trace in his book. His conclusion, a conclusion that I myself have often promoted, was that if we want to be educated in the highest things, we will probably not be able to find such an education in existing academic institutions insofar as these are premised on the philosophical premises of modernity. So our situation is rather more perplexing than that of the classic Greeks

In his *Closing of the American Mind,* Allan Bloom said that the saddest and unhappiest people in the country today were the students at the best and most expensive schools. They were unhappy because they were assured that they were receiving the best education possible, but, on receiving it, they found it was immanently boring and narrow. None of the really great things were brought up, except in some relativistic context that prevented any ultimate solution to any question, no matter how urgent.

Thus, following on Voegelin and Schumacher, the question is: To where does the mind flee if the city and the academy are both disordered? In one sense, we can contend that revelation was designed to deal with this issue in a number of ways, principally by correcting or completing the poets and the philosophers without denying the truths that they learned from insight and true argument. But by any empirical standards, we would be loathe to maintain that academic institutions under the general aegis of the Church are immune from the problems coming from the city or the academy. Nor are they completely open to considerations that might come from revelation itself.

IV.

In this context, let me return to John Paul II's document of 1989. The Pope noticed that one of the main problems with universities is a lack of a proper criterion about what might be of more or less importance. "There is a crisis resulting from so many ideologies and models of conduct which in the changing scene of today and which have left many people without identity and without any existential certainty."[3] Our problem is not too little knowledge but, paradoxically, too much, or at least too much knowledge that is not adequately sorted out and ordered. The real problem, as St. Thomas told beginners in the Prologue of the *Summa,* is disordered knowledge.

The university is not just something to train us to be participants in the work force, though that is not an ignoble purpose. Nor

3   Ibid., p. 262.

will new programs and new departments solve a university's problem with its own soul. The Pope goes to the heart of the matter:

> The challenge touches on more basic questions. What is at stake is *the very meaning of scientific and technological research*, of society, of culture; on a more profound level, what is at stake is *the very meaning of man* . . . . We can say that the challenges have to do with the truth about man in his personal and social dimension; about the world with its laws which have to be discovered and put to use for the good of humanity; and the *truth about God*, the foundation of being, to whom all is to lead and who *alone* gives ultimate meaning to man and to the world. These are *questions which are proper to the university* world, and with which universities must concern themselves, since the proper role of the university is that of probing, going to the root of the problem.[4]

The two problems that Voegelin touched on, "Why is there something, not nothing?" and "Why is this thing this thing and not that thing?" are likewise implicit in John Paul II's observation. The pope does not hesitate to affirm that "the truth about God" is crucial to the "proper meaning of man." If universities do not inquire about such issues, then they will flee the university to find a home in other institutions and endeavors.

A theme that seems to characterize peculiarly Catholic reflections on the university is, or should be, the question of truth itself, the very fact that we can and must use this word. To ask of the "truth of things" is not a forbidden question. We do not begin in or assume relativism as if it is the governing philosophic position of university life, though we can understand it and hence subject it also to the criterion of truth. "I am thinking, therefore, about the truth as something researched, loved, taught, and promulgated," John Paul continued. "This is the heart and soul of the university, because

---

4 Ibid., p. 263.

it is the source of life for human reason: '*Perfectio intellectus est verum,*' Truth is the perfection of the intellect.' says St. Thomas (*Contra Gentiles*, III, 51)."[5] Truth seems to have a certain underlying impetus of its own—"something researched, loved, taught, and promulgated." When found, it is not something we can leave alone.

Truth, when it appears at all, often appears as fragmented and even composed of contradictory elements. "There is general and widespread evidence today that unity of knowledge has been lost in the area of university research . . . . The university is meant to be a 'living unity' of individual organisms dedicated to the research into truth."[6] The Holy Father's emphasis on a common orientation of all research and knowledge toward truth is not just a peculiar Polish aberration, as if it were somehow culturally conditioned. It reveals something in the very nature of man.

It is necessary to work a higher synthesis of knowledge, in which alone lies the possibility of satisfying that *thirst for truth* which is profoundly inscribed on the heart of the human person. Augustine expresses this well: "*Quid enim fortius desiderat anima quam veritatem*" ('What is there that the soul desires more strongly than truth?', Augustine Commentary on John, 265). While other creatures exist without any knowledge of the 'why,' man with his intelligence is the protagonist of the ongoing search for the 'why.' . . . The 'why' or the 'whys' are ever present within the fundamental questions of the human spirit . . . . And it is *his passionate* need *for the truth* which leads to a passionate search for the authentic good of humanity.[7]

Such words again recall Plato, the philosophic *eros* for truth. The analogies are physical "thirst," "desire," "searchings." "Why" is

5   Ibid., p. 263.
6   Ibid., p. 263.
7   Ibid., p. 264.

located in our very being, but not as something that can never be answered. Our need for truth is precisely "passionate" and as such leads us to look for the real good of our kind.

V.

To the vexing question of what does revelation add to a university, such that it would be incomplete without it, the Pope remarks,

> The means that the Catholic university uses the same as those of any other university. However, in the conduct of its academic research, it can rely on a superior enlightenment which, without changing the nature of this research, purifies it, orients it, enriches it and uplifts it. It is *the light of faith, the light of Christ*, who has said "I am the Way, the Truth, and the Life." This light is not found "outside" of *rational research*, as a limitation or an impediment, but rather "above" it, as its elevation and an expansion of its horizons. The light of faith opens the way to the completion of truth.[8]

These words foreshadow *Fides et Ratio*. Revelation does not replace philosophy or science. Yet the very fact that they do not complete themselves leads to a certain wonder if their completion is addressed to us in another way. It is not "outside" of rational research that its limits are found, but within them. These are remarkable words—that there may be a "way" to the "completion of truth." We can choose to close off this way, no doubt, but that very closing off would itself be a sin against the light of mind itself.

E. F. Schumacher also had noticed that there were certain problems that were not finished once and for all, but had to be repeated as solutions in every soul and in every culture. Schumacher thought that economics as a science that enabled us to know how to provide for our material needs was already known. If these needs were not

8   Ibid., 264–65.

met by known means, it was not, strictly, an economic problem. The Pope touches on this same point: "The problem of human development, beginning with those least fortunate, is much more an ethical problem than a technical one."[9] This was also the Platonic point, that the disorders of the external world are first disorders of our souls, and not vice versa.

Cardinal Stafford, in a comment at Ave Maria Law School, touched upon the philosophic and theological insights of thinkers like Alasdair MacIntyre, Charles Taylor, and Tracy Rowland, who frequently pointed out that culture is never neutral. While there may be good things in any culture, things to be sought out and affirmed, still there were within cultures, and not just the "culture of death" in our own culture to which the Holy Father often refers, things that had to be rejected or corrected. This was in fact one of the functions of revelation as it relates to human culture.

The Pope had already alluded to this question in his 1989 address: "The Catholic university must recognize the dignity and creativity within the various cultures of the world, but at the same time be committed to their purification and elevation through the light and active force of the Gospel—a process which in no way sacrifices what is authentically human; whatever is truly valid is developed and brought to complete and fruitful reality."[10] Revelation, in this sense, is not simply "neutral" in any culture. This may be why so many nations and cultures today restrict it, prevent it from the simple freedom of being what it is. It too is probably the seed of a much more widespread martyrdom that goes on in the modern world than we are wont to acknowledge, something that Robert Royal pointed out in his *Catholic Martyrs of the Twentieth Century*.

Years ago (1979), the Daughters of St. Paul published an early collection of addresses that the then new Pope, John Paul II, gave to "university students and faculties." It was striking in these early days to me as the editor of this volume, how at home the young

9   Ibid., p. 265.
10 Ibid., p. 265.

Pope was in the university settings that he often seemed to seek out and which, in turn, seemed to seek him out. That collection was entitled, "the whole truth about man." Some ten years later, John Paul II repeated the same theme: "But the *supreme criterion*, in whose light the Catholic university must measure all its options, remains *Christ, the Incarnate Word* who is *the full truth about man.*"[11] I would emphasize the importance of this sentence about "the full truth about man" in the context of a university culture in which Christ is too frequently presented merely as an "inspired" man, or a "leader" of the oppressed, or as a community developer, anything but the Incarnate Word, the dimensions of whose being constitute the foundation both of what is made in the Word and in the Word made flesh.

Modern intellectual relativism has the indirect effect of minimizing the importance of thought, let alone accurate thought. Ellis Sandoz, in his fine book on Dostoevesky's Grand Inquisitor, recently reissued, has again recalled the problematic of modern atheism and its spiritual roots. The Holy Father was quite aware of this background:

> On this subject (religious indifferentism and atheism) it (the Catholic University) must have the courage to speak a truth which is not convenient, a truth which does not flatter, but a truth which is absolutely necessary in order to safeguard the true dignity of the human person. It must remind the world of culture that, while it is surely true that men and women can organize the world *without God*, but without God it will, in the last analysis, be organized *against humanity*.

11   Ibid., p. 265.

Chapter 6

THE READING ROOM[*]

On Being "Troubled" by the Immensity

of Things To Be Known

The sea will have swept over it (writing in the sand), even as time rolls its effacing waves over the names of statesmen and warriors and poets. Hark! The surf-wave laughs at you. Passing from the beach, I begin to clamber over the crags, making my difficult way among the ruins of a rampart shattered and broken by the assaults of a fierce enemy. The rocks rise in every variety of attitude. Some of them have their feet in the foam and are shagged halfway upwards with seaweed; some have been hollowed almost into caverns by the unwearied toil of the sea, which can afford to spend centuries in wearing away a rock, or even polishing a pebble. One huge rock ascends in monumental shape, with a face like a giant's tombstone, on which the veins resemble inscriptions, but in an unknown language. We will fancy them the forgotten characters of an antediluvian race, or else that Nature's own hand has here recorded a mystery which, could I read her language, would make mankind the wiser and the happier. *How many a thing has troubled me with that same idea!* Pass on and leave it unexplained."
— Nathaniel Hawthorne, "Footprints on the Seashore."[1]

---

*   Lecture given at the Intercollegiate Studies Institute, Wilmington, Delaware, September 11, 2008.

1   Nathaniel Hawthorne, "Footprints on the Seashore," *Twice-Told Tales* (New York: David McKay, 1891), p. 439.

"Omne ens est verum." (Everything *that is* is true).
— St. Thomas Aquinas.

I.

When I first taught at the Gregorian University in Rome in 1965, the Library of the University had a huge central Sala in the center of which were arranged large, handsome wooden tables that could sit maybe ten or so scholars each. This Library was the more modern version of the Library of the sixteenth-century *Collegio Romano*, now brought into the twentieth century after the Vatican-Italian pacts of 1929. Formerly, the *Collegio Romano* was next to the Church of San Ignazio, but now relocated under the Quirinale, next to the Colonna Gardens in Piazza della Pilotta, located between the Piazza Venezia and the Trevi Fountains. The modern library, though it lost many of its classical works when the Italian state took over the earlier school, was itself impressive. It contained books in most ancient and modern academic languages.

In earlier ages, no professor or student could take a book from the library. One had to read in the Library. Only professors could use this library. Books were precious and personal copies rare. Students recorded what the professors read in the Library. By the time I arrived in Rome, if one was a professor, as I was, he could obtain a key that enabled him to enter the library day or night to read whatever he liked. Moreover, a professor could check out books and take them to his room. This privilege was a rather modern innovation. Previously, books had to be kept at the tables and used there. As an American, I was already used to the paper-back revolution that enabled almost anyone to own many inexpensive books. The larger library was a kind of back-up for things one did not possess.

All of this reading room etiquette stems from before computers came to be with on-line books and journals whereby the library is almost literally brought into one's room or with cell phone type instruments into one's automobile or on one's walk. Recently, I was in a car in Santa Monica with two ex-students and their parents. I had mentioned the very excellent on-line home-studies program that Peter Redpath put together, but I could not remember its name. In about a minute, one of my young friends had looked it up on a cell-phone in the back seat of the moving car. Printed books, of course, in the history of mankind, are relatively recent, five centuries or so. Prior to that are manuscript carefully written by hand on hide or parchment, or chiseled on stone tablets. Everyone relied much more on memory and oral presentations. Memory is often a rather lost but still valuable art.

But a "reading room" in which almost everyone has been in at one time or another is the image that I want to keep in mind here. I like the idea of a man or woman sitting at a desk quietly absorbed in reading a book. Meantime, the reader is surrounded by other readers likewise absorbed. On all sides of the reading room are shelves holding volumes of every sort, size, or configuration. The reading rooms at the Library of Congress in Washington only make this image more graphic as that Library is so enormous. Its aim is nothing less than to collect everything collectable so that, should someone want to find an item in any language or from any era or any place, it will be there. Someone, sometime might want to know what it says. Once someone somewhere has written something, however obscure, we want to keep it, just in case, as Hawthorne said, it will contribute to making us "wiser and happier."

Actually, today almost everything is on-line in some form or another. We can have a small instrument in our hands or attached to our ears from which can be picked up all this information, whirling invisibly about us in the air at all times and places. We think of all the radio and television stations in the world beaming their signals through our very bodies. With these instruments, once so large, now so small, we are able to receive and direct our understanding to anything on-line. Technology has succeeded in making everything available to every one at all times and in all places. In this world, the distinction of day and night disappears. The reading room doors are always open if we choose to enter.

We think of a company like Netflix, which evidently can make available to us almost any movie that was ever produced in any language. Much of the music that has ever been composed we can find and hear. Instrumental music already transcends the diversity of languages. We are no longer bound by the "latest" movie or song. Old time radio can give us Jack Benny as easily as it can give us the evening news. Moreover, this information is not restricted to our planet. We a have a constant radio watch on our planet for those sending signals from outer-space that may indicate someone out there is trying to contact us, some other rational being. The size and complexity of outer space are matched by the tininess and order of inner space that we find within ourselves and within the things we know.

II.

It is not my purpose here to give an up-to-date description of the latest in information technology. Libraries sometimes refer to call themselves today as "information centers," a mistake, I think. The cell phone, the standard and mini-computers are everywhere. The poor have them and some politician will no doubt invent a "right" to them. An old Latin phrase talked of *omne ens scibile*, every thing is knowable. What is remarkable is that we are surrounded by a superabundance of things about which we are, for some strange reason, curious. The curiosity may be as mysterious as the existence of things to be curious about. The sheer size of the universe astonishes us insofar as we can even comprehend it.

Yet, in spite of its size and evident complexity, we seek to know the vast world, where it came from, what it is about. We definitely know some things about it. The cosmos, moreover, does not seek to know us, unless perhaps there are other finite intelligent beings somewhere out there. Some scientists take their existence as certain; others doubt it. But no evidence is so far found in either case. We are surrounded also by an immensity of things that we do know about. The knowledge is of the things themselves. But the things are not "knowledge" which is its own reality. This accumulated knowledge is preserved in words, in books, and in technical systems. But such knowledge is only alive when we actually know what is in such sources. The thing known seems much more "alive" when it is actually being known.

A two-hundred-and-fifty-page book, whatever its content, is a solid, firm thing. We can pick it up, carry it about, weigh it. But that same book on-line is but a blip as we ship a copy of it across the world almost instantaneously while we yet keep it for ourselves. Still, it is not a mere blip when we manage to retrieve it, stretch it out, and perhaps print it on paper, so that we can read it and understand it. All the books in the world and all the blips of information in cyberspace are simply facts until they are known by someone with a mind that can relate them to everything else.

The word "information," just knowing and identifying things, is by no means equivalent to the word "wisdom." Yet wisdom includes "word." It includes how all things knowingly fit together. It includes wonderment about why things are rather than are not, why something is this way, not that. When we think, we distinguish and classify things. We give them names. We write what we know; others can read with we write. True knowledge seems to belong to anyone if he would but do what is necessary to learn it.

In some sense, we can say that the world is, and ought to be, reproduced in words. We do not think that the vast variety of languages speak of different worlds or of different things. They address the same world in different words that can be understood once we know the language. We can point to what we are talking about no matter what language we use to call attention to what we point to. Reproduction of spoken into written words is, however, itself static until the words themselves are actually being known and used in a mind in conversation with other knowers.

The knowing of words, however, should not make us think that in knowing *the things that are* as words, we do not also know the reality to which they point. We know both the words and the reality that they designate. We might die for our friend or country. We do not die for the word, friend, or country, except in the sense of keeping the meaning of words so that we may know one another at all. The deliberate lie destroys the purpose of words. The account of the Tower of Babel in which no one could understand another's language was a disaster that did not change the world itself or the things in it to be named.

What is this thing we call "mind?" Is it just another "thing" alongside other things? We do not bump up against minds in the streets, only people with minds. A book is just another thing when it is sitting on our desk unopened. But mind is the functioning of a certain quality within a thing, a human thing, or perhaps anything with mind. Minds without bodies are at least conceivable as we know from Socrates last speech in the *Apology*.

The activity of mind goes on within a cosmos of things themselves capable of being known. It is a remarkable phenomenon, the two worlds, things and mind, that are yet in our world. That is to say, the world of things is not complete without the world of words that designate them in the minds of those beings who converse with one another, who write so that others can know the truth of things.

The world of the mind includes the accurate effort to state what it is that we encounter in reality. It also includes the things we, as it were, "sub-create," to use Tolkien's happy phrase, namely, our stories, our imaginations, our wonder about the things that might have been but are not, yet are imagined, written about. Our own lives are not complete or even tolerable if they include only our own experiences. We need to "live" lives that are not our own even to live our own lives fully and fruitfully. We speak of virtual or vicarious reality almost as if we might prefer it to the reality that we know exists apart from ourselves. Ivan Karamazov did not exist, yet his literary existence is included in the existence by which we understand ourselves. We know his story.

Not all things have minds, of course. But things with minds range over all things, even those without minds. Things without minds are none the less knowable. They indicate mind by their being at all, by their being this not that. This is what the phrase that I used in the beginning from Aquinas via Aristotle, "*omne ens est verum*," means. The classic definition of mind is that power within a rational being whereby it is capable of "knowing all things." Such a power evidently existed before it was positively known to exist by the human beings that came to know it. In other words, it did not cause itself to be mind or to be activated by attending to other things not itself. Our minds begin with knowing things, things with matter, with what our senses, themselves also constitutive of our very being, reveal to us. We are, it is said, the lowest of the beings with intelligence. God, it is said, knows all things by knowing Himself. We only know things already made, already not ourselves.

Yet, we say that no single finite human being knows all things. We doubt if all of us put together know all things. We suspect that having many knowers is a good thing. But our not knowing may be the result of something else, lack of opportunity, perhaps, time, or even interest. And it is probably not correct to say that the mind "knows." Rather it is with our minds that we affirm that we know what is not ourselves. We must at some point say "I know" in order for knowing to be actual. Truth, as Robert Sokolowski often says, needs an agent. This mind that we possess seems curious to us. It seems initially to have nothing within it except itself. This means it can be what it is not while remaining itself. Knowledge can be defined as "being what one is not." Thus knowing solves that ancient question of why is it all right to be ourselves. It is because, with minds, we do not miss out on that myriad of things that are not ourselves.

We notice that we do not know ourselves as knowing until we know what is not ourselves. Ironically, something else has to "give" us what is necessary for us to know what we are. We discover precisely ourselves while we look back reflexively on the fact that it is "I" who knows what is not myself. The what-is-not-ourselves that incites us to know at all, is, in fact, *anything that is*. But two people can know the same thing that is not one or the other of them. They can then talk about it. This convergence must mean that something is common to the things known and to the different people who know it.

We not only use our minds practically to make things like poems and bridges, but also to know one another. The knowing of someone else takes place through the exchange of words about the reality that each of the conversing persons has in common. At some point, the knowing of someone else involves the wanting to be known by someone else. The one known must choose to be known, to reveal himself. This is what Aristotle's discussions of friendship were really about.

III.

Reading rooms bring us to books, but we have to decide to go there, take down a book, open it up. Books bring us to ideas, to stories, to facts, to truths. But we have to read them, think about them. An artist once exclaimed, on finishing a painting, "Now, here's *the* picture—one of my best too—I've just finished. When I started out I had no idea what it was going to be." On hearing this explanation, his logical friend replied, "After you got through, how did you find out what it was?" No better example of Aristotle's notion of practical intellect could be found. Practical truth is the conformity of what we produce with what we intend to produce. The configuration of matter into words follows the guidance of intellect through the hand. Paintings are given names, even odd ones. Because the artist, having finished, did know what it was. He names it. The naming of things is essential to our knowing them.

Thus, there is truth in this amusing reply. The "truth" of a story or poem or essay is not fully seen when the author begins. He only fully knows what he says or draws when he has brought his idea forth. But this bringing forth is under the guidance of his mind. Tolkien, I think, found out about the fate of Bilbo and Frodo by writing about them. He did not know the end of the story until he arrived at it. He did now know, from the beginning, that great events are dependent on people no one else would notice. We are capable of imitating the divinity in this sense. How did the artist know what it was? By reading his own story or seeing his own picture. He made a thing that did not exist come to be. But it was he who guided the story with his own mind, who put the flesh on it.

Somehow, even "nonsense" rhymes have a point to them. All of our humor depends on seeing connection in things that seem not to be connected or connected in an odd way. Our humor is almost the most starting proof of our rationality, of our ability to see connections and contrasts. Humor is a measure of our intelligence. There is no laugher without a mind that holds together the things that cause its intelligibility. If we do not "get" a joke, we do not laugh. Getting jokes is itself a primary sign of rationality, the rationally that can see reason in what does not seem rational or orderly.

In the beginning, I cited something from Hawthorne's short story, "Footprints on the Seashore." He sees many remarkable things on the shore, things just there, including his own or another's footprints. He thinks, fleetingly, that he sees something in them that will make "mankind wiser and happier," perhaps an ancient tongue or nature's own wordings. One can hardly blame anyone for such a search that is recalled to us by seeing what is on a seashore. We have wondered about these reminders of ourselves on other shores, in other times. Hawthorne then draws the universal principle behind his musings: "How many a thing has troubled me with this same idea!" Hawthorne uses the very graphic word "troubled." We are troubled" that we are not wiser and happier. We should be both, we think. And it is not just one thing that causes in us this troublement. "How many a thing"—everything *that is*—can cause the same troubling of our spirit?

Presumably, we would not be "troubled" if we were already "wiser and happier." If we are not in fact wise and happy, we think we should be. Where do we get this idea? Most of us have heard of the Garden of Eden or the City of God. We know of the City in Speech and of Utopia. In the history of modern philosophy, we can make a rather strong case for the fact that it has been precisely the learned theories about how to make us "wiser and happier" that have been most disastrous for our kind. Theories of progress and classless societies are but philosophical intimations of this same unsettling and troubling thought. We search for both grandiose and for personal answers. Some philosophers want us to transform the universe; others advise us to begin first with ourselves.

What is the vision that Hawthorne provides for us here? We

are walking on the beach. We see the footprints in the sand. They quickly are washed away, never to return again. This experience of fleetingness, of fragility, is next compared to our memories of great statesmen and writers of the past whom we have quickly forgotten. We should not forget them. If we forget them, what they stood for will also be forgotten. Evidently, the forgetfulness of history troubles us. We once knew; now we have forgotten. We are not beings who can remember everything. Yet without memory we could not be the kind of beings we are. We need help.

We have libraries, the storehouses of memory. The amount of collective memory contained in libraries is enormous. We recall the oft-repeated phrase that "he who forgets history will be condemned to repeat it." Yet, we know nothing can really be "repeated." The old cyclic notion of history thought it could. We find cyclic history in the Romans and in the Greeks. Indeed, that repetition is what gave intelligibility to history itself. We could learn from its lessons. But this learning from history meant that we had or could have some effect on our own history. What happened also depended on what we did, what we wanted to happen and took steps to make happen.

Reading rooms have signs in them: "Quiet!" "Do Not Disturb!" We can detect a sequence, from silence to conversation and back to silence. Learning is an activity that we must engage in ourselves. Yet, it is characteristic of knowing that we want to tell someone about it. What goes on in our souls seems to be intended for other souls. Yet this experience itself leads to further awe, to the contemplation together of *all that is*. We sometimes think that the highest act of our intellect is to know the truth. No doubt this is a high order of inner life. But truth is expressed in word. Truth leads not so much to itself but to praise and celebration.

Celebration is not for the reading room, though that is probably its origin, in the quiet pursuit of our knowing *what is*. All celebration indeed begins in truth, in the knowing and rejoicing in the things that we are not. Celebration is expressed, as Plato says in the *Laws*, in singing and dancing and sacrificing. We celebrate only when the end is achieved, when the victory is won, the game is over.

All existence seems to point to a final celebration about which, as Hawthorne intimated, we sometimes have inklings on seashores or in dining with our friends.

We might say that the reading room leads to the dining table. The dining table leads to the concert hall or the dance floor. The concert hall and the dance floor lead to the Church. The reading room is where we contemplate. The dining room is where we converse. The concert hall is where we listen to what is beautiful. The Church is where we celebrate the existence in which we are already caught up and to that transcendence to which it points by being *what is it*. Just as our very existence is not something we give ourselves, so our final celebration is likewise give to us. What really makes us "wiser and happier" is not of our making. The freedom of the self is ordered finally to the freedom of God, to what finally we are given, not to what we make, however wondrous that may be.

Of late, after having read the passage a hundred times, I saw the following lines of Aristotle: "If the gods give any gift at all to human beings, it is reasonable for them to give happiness also; indeed, it is reasonable to give happiness more than any other human good, in so far as it is the basis of human goods." I leave you with this thought: "Did the gods finally make this 'reasonable' gift?" The great lesson we take away from our reading rooms is why we are led by our philosophy to questions we must ask but cannot answer. To conclude with the next sentence of Aristotle: "Presumably, this question is more suitable for a different inquiry." As we look about our reading room, we ask ourselves whether there are books on the shelves that deal with this "different inquiry."

Chapter 7

On Teaching and the Highest Good[*]

We do not hold the common view that a man's highest good is to survive and simply continue to exist. His highest good is to become as virtuous as possible and to continue to exist in that state as long as life lasts.
— Plato, *The Laws*, IV, 347 B. C., #707d.

Every man is, or hopes to be, an *Idler*. Even those who seem to differ most from us are hastening to increase our Fraternity; as peace is the end of war, so to be idle is the ultimate purpose of the busy."
— Samuel Johnson, *The Idler*, No. 1, Saturday, 15 April 1758.[1]

Publius Cornelius Scipio, the first of his family to be called Africanus, used to remark that he was never less idle than when he had nothing to do, and never less lonely than when he was by himself.
— Cicero, *De Officiis*, I, 44 B. C.[2]

I.

First of all, I am honored and pleased to receive an honorary degree from this small and excellent college in the State of New Hampshire.

*   Commencement Address, Thomas More College, Merrimack, New Hampshire, May, 2008. Published in *Vital Speeches*, LXIV (July 2008), pp. 326–29.
1   *Selected Essays* (Harmondsworth: Penguin, 2003), p. 407.
2   *Selected Works* (Harmondsworth: Penguin, 1971), p. 159.

I have been here before, in the winter of 2001, midst piles of snow all about. At that time, I gave a lecture entitled: "Modernity: What Is It? Must We Adopt It?" This lecture eventually became a chapter in my book, *Roman Catholic Political Philosophy*. Modernity is a topic to which I often return. I recall from my previous visit that the whole student body dressed formally for the lecture. This same student body served the meals, perhaps a portent of Johnson's relationship between busy-ness and idleness, or Aristotle's practical and contemplative life.

What to speak about to a graduating class of Thomas More College presents, I confess, something of a challenge. I suspect, under the tutelage of Peter Sampo and Jeffrey Nelson, that students here are already familiar with Schall's favorite themes, the themes of our civilization itself. But the main justification of a relatively new college like Thomas More is that, when sorted out, it is a place where one will learn things that are simply are not found in most other institutions or not found so well reflected. Schools of "higher learning" do not always devote much time to the "highest things." The "highest things" is a phrase that is often used in today's academia, a kind of parody of the Second Commandment, to avoid using the actual name of the Lord. But it is a useful phrase for all that.

I have begun this short talk by citing three classical references. The first from Plato asks about man's highest good. The second from Samuel Johnson recalls Aristotle's dictum that the purpose of work is not itself work, but leisure. And the third citation, from Cicero, tells us that our most intense activity may come, perhaps can only come, when we are alone. And this "activity," that takes place when we are capable of being alone with ourselves, always consists in knowing and reflecting first on what is not ourselves. It is the very purpose of intelligence that what is not ourselves becomes ourselves after our manner of knowing.

Aristotle asked much the same question of God, namely, "Is He lonely?" Revelation tells us that God is not alone even when He is alone. At the inner essence of the Godhead is otherness of persons, whether the otherness of creation exists or not. Our human "being," made in the image of God, reminds us of this transcendent origin of *all that* is, especially when we are alone, though not lonely. The existence of all things not God is never fully explained by themselves. What is not God does not exist because God needs what is not Himself to be what He is.

On Whitsunday in 1925, Belloc tells us, in his *Towns of Destiny*, that he was in the Cathedral of Narbonne in southern France. "We are bound," he reminds us, "upon a very different journey from that of this world." We too seek the "highest things" that may not finally be located within this world even though we do journey in this world.

Saying this, Belloc looks up at the High Altar in the Cathedral. "Well then, the Mass began." Thus, he brings us right into the sacred action itself, the one action that is the same sacrifice wherever it recurs in time or place.

> They bore above the head of the celebrant priest that round shade of silk which had also come centuries and centuries ago from Rome. They had their particular rites of the bishopric, and of their tradition. They read the Gospel, not from the altar steps, but from high up near the roof, above the heads of the whole people; from the organ loft, in splendid fashion. And when they sang the *Veni Creator*, I could swear that the light which fell in the place took on another quality.[3]

We can see it, can't we? The Cathedral of Narbonne, the reading of the Gospel from high up, on Whitsunday, the Episcopal rites, the beautiful *Veni Creator Spiritus*. We do look on this world with a light that gives our places "another quality." This is what it means to believe, to know the truth that makes us free in a place wherein it might be found.

3   Hilaire Belloc, *Towns of Destiny* (New York: Robert M. McBride, MCMXXVII), p. 228.

II.

A grand-niece of mine, who works as a civilian for Navy Intelligence, recently sent me the following remark of Abraham Lincoln, a remark I do not recall ever having seen before: "Nearly all men can handle adversity," Lincoln wrote, "but if you want to test a man's character, give him power." In the *Laws* of Plato, the Athenian Stranger, as you recall, tells the Spartan and the Cretan gentlemen that the real thing that tests man's virtue is not war, which only tests courage, but peace, which tests all virtues. "What to do when not at war?" is the central moral question. The end of war is peace. The activities of peace, if we do not know what they are, are much more dangerous to civilization than the activities of war. Peace is not an "end" to be chosen. "Peace studies," as such, are generally useless if not dangerous. Peace is, as Augustine said, the "tranquility of order." The order, which results in tranquility, must first be known and chosen and put into our lives and polities.

This recollection of Lincoln, however, reminded me of something from Allan Bloom that I read every semester with my students. He wrote:

> When Sextus Pompeius is given the chance of murdering his guests and becoming emperor of the universe or remaining within the pale of decency and being done away with himself, we are confronted with a classic problem of political morality, one that is presented with detail and precision in *Anthony and Cleopatra*. We must recognize it as such, and we must further have some knowledge of the kinds of men who desire to rule and of what this desire does to them.[4]

What does this desire for power do to us? I take it students at this college will not be surprised that something profound can be learned by reading *Anthony and Cleopatra*.

---

4   Allan Bloom, *Shakespeare's Politics* (Chicago: University of Chicago Press, 1964), p. 11.

The purpose of literature, which exists first for its own sake, is to enable us find out things that we need to know but things that we may never have yet experienced in our own world before we need them. Literature, to which this college is devoted, allows us to live more lives than our own, however broad or limited our own lives may be. Literature and biography also prepare us to know what happens or might happen in the souls of others when they choose to pursue the various ends open to their souls, one of which ends, as Aristotle said, is precisely power and the honor that goes with it.

Moreover, we can only know what happens in the souls of others if we know our own souls and what can happen, might happen, to them, if we so choose and allow it. We are not to be overly surprised by evil even if we be not vicious ourselves. Ignorance about the darker side of the human condition and what may be expected of it is not a virtue.

III.

College, and this is an admittedly counter-cultural opinion, ought to be imagined as a group of buildings surrounded by high walls. These ramparts are designed to prevent, for a time, the students within from fondly looking horizontally to the immediate world of their time. This freedom from the pressure of the present that such walls provide frees the students, even from themselves, so that they can, at least at a brief time in their short lives, look upwards not merely sideways. We are, hopefully, to be protected from the scourge of immediate relevance so that we might consider things that are for their own sakes, lest we miss them in our busy-ness. Few universities, to be sure, see this kind of openness as their primary or even secondary purpose.

Russell Berman, in his new book, *Fiction Sets You Free*, writes: "It is surely curious that society devotes any resources to the circulation of mere fictions. There is nothing obvious about this constant habit of telling tales whose essential nature is precisely their lack of empirical truth or informational content."[5] Fiction can only be

---

5   Russell Berman, *Fiction Sets You Free: Literature, Liberty, and Western Culture* (Iowa City: University of Iowa Press, 2007), p. xi.

true by not being true in its immediate details of time and place. One indeed might say with Tolkien, that the world looks upon Christianity as a "tale," a "myth" that not only cannot be historically true, but cannot be philosophically cogent. Christianity, of course, looks on itself as the one "tale" that is literally true because it is not merely a tale. The Word was made flesh and did dwell amongst us. Our tales have dates and places.

To found and attend a college named after Thomas More, the man who recalls Plato in his writing of *Utopia*, strikes me in our day as an act of, yes, courage. Courage, as we recall, is the virtue most associated with war. However, as we remember from the *Republic*, Socrates praised Adeimantus and Glaucon, Plato's brothers, above all for their courage.

But by courage, the first virtue, Socrates did not mean only courage in war, though he meant that too. Socrates himself showed courage in the battles of Delium, Potidea, and Amphipolis in which he fought. He praised the brothers for the courage to want to understand when they knew they did not grasp something. At the trial of Christ, we have much contempt for the Roman Governor who, on asking the most basic of all questions, namely, "What is truth?" did not have the courage to wait around for an answer.

Socrates praised Adeimantus and Glaucon for making such a logical argument for injustice but even more for their suspecting their own sophisticated argument was incorrect. This correction of our ideas is why we ever want to talk to Socrates, the philosopher. Socrates stands at the heart of our civilization and indeed, as I think, of civilization itself. The central principle of civilization, which Christianity explicitly reaffirms in the death of Christ, is, as we read in the *Apology*, that it is "never right to do wrong." Much of modern thought from at least Machiavelli is designed to deny this principle in order to set us "free" to define our own good, a freedom that allows us to do what is evil if we will it.

In the *Laches*, the dialogue involves Nicias and other men, including Socrates himself, who were soldiers in the Peloponnesian War. As he constantly does, Socrates seeks to extend the scope of each virtue so that it includes its proper place within all virtues. He says to Laches, himself an Athenian general concerned about the education of his son,

> I wanted to learn from you not only what constitutes courage for a hoplite but for a horseman as well and for every sort of warrior. And I wanted to include not only those who are courageous in warfare but also those who are brave in dangers at sea, and the ones who show courage in illness and poverty and affairs of state; and then again I wanted to include not only those who are brave in the face of pain and fear but also those who are clever at fighting desire and pleasure, whether by standing their ground or running away—because there are some men, aren't there, Laches, who are brave in matters like these? (191d-e).

There are some, Socrates says, who are "brave" in matters such as these, in matters of desire and pleasure, in matters of truth. The walls of a true university, if I might put it that way, allow us to understand courage in this Socratic sense of courage as a virtue of peace that incites us to speak the truth even if it is not permitted to exist in our polities, be they tyrannical or democratic. It is no accident in these days that it is the popes who are most concerned with precisely "democratic tyranny."

IV.

Let me conclude. Number 272 of Pascal's *Pensées* reads: "There is nothing so conformable to reason as this disavowal of reason." Indeed, one might say that the only protection we have against reason is to disavow its instrumentality, its ability to get us to reality, to *what is*. You have hopefully noticed during your stay here the remarkable attention to reason, to its methods, nature, and limits that has flourished in recent times within Catholicism. We often hear the notions of mystery and reason played off against each other. Reason is said to want to overcome the mysteries; mysticism is said to be unreasonable.

The Catholic idea of mystery is not that the mystery which is the Godhead does not want itself known to us. Just the opposite, the whole purpose of revelation is precisely that we understand that the Word is made flesh. Our problem is not a lack of light but too much light. We are not, thankfully, gods. Yet we are open to what does not originate in ourselves. Indeed, we do not originate in ourselves, nor do the things we most long to know.

When a student finishes college at the age of twenty-one or twenty-two, he should know, as Plato taught, that he is not yet old enough, not yet experienced enough really to know what it is that we are about. It is often said that the end of college is the beginning of a more full life. And this is true. But it is also the beginning of a realization that our lives point beyond themselves as do all the things we really know. Nothing that we know fully explains itself. Once we understand this, we begin the true adventure of what it is to be a human being in this world. It is not to be forgotten that the two human beings who are most fundamental to understanding what we are, Christ and Socrates, never wrote a book. Both were killed by the best states in their time in a legal trial. Both thought that those who followed them would probably experience in some way the same fate.

Socrates died telling us: "No evil could harm a good man," not even death itself. Indeed, death was to be preferred to doing evil. Christ died commending His spirit to the Father and forgiving His enemies. Socrates often taught his greatest lessons in stories, parables, or "myths." Christianity is said to be the one "myth" that is true. It is comforting to disavow reason that we might not have to face the truth. But the real and only adventure is to face the truth.

So let the last words you hear at Thomas More College be those that many of you may be familiar with from your youth. They are words mindful of those I cited in the beginning from Plato, Johnson, and Cicero.

"Then the prophecies of the old songs have turned out to be true, after a fashion!" said Bilbo.

"Of course!" said Gandolf. "And why should not they prove true? Surely you don't disbelieve the prophecies, because you had a hand in bringing them about yourself? You don't really suppose, do you, that all your adventures and escapes were managed by mere luck, just for your sole benefit? You are a very fine person, Mr. Baggins, and I am very fond of you; but you are only quite a little fellow in a wide world after all."

"Thank goodness!" said Bilbo laughing and handed him the tobacco-jar.

The walls of the college exist so that we can hear such things, and on hearing them, likewise give thanks that we have actually, in our silence, heard them and the truths that go with them.

Chapter 8

READING WITHOUT LEARNING[*]

On Not Missing "Sublime Passages"

I.

When graduation week arrives, the perennial question comes up: "What did our students get for their education money during their high school or college years?" No one, as far as I can tell, thinks anyone is getting too much, whatever too much of knowing might mean. And I know that we cannot measure in economic terms what we are supposed to learn in school at whatever level. Moreover, if we do use this economic criterion, we know that what we measure by such means is not what we most need to know.

Still, the question is not frivolous. Even if intangible, something is supposed to happen in our souls in college or graduate school, something that makes us more human, more of what we are supposed to be, being what we already are. As Professor E. O. Hirsh has pointed out,[1] it does seem possible systematically to teach children how to pronounce words, and in this sense how to read and write, without their ever actually coming to learn anything from their reading.

Indeed, this separation of content and method seems to be the preferred way, so that educational tests seek to measure "reading" as opposed to "reading what?" After a few months or years of instruction on this premise, it turns out, in survey after survey, that students, who apparently know how to read, do not read much. Hirsch makes the marvelous, counter-intuitive comment that the

---

[*] This essay was originally published on-line by Ignatius Insight, May 2006.
[1] *Education Week*, April 26, 2006.

best way to incite students to read is to give them something worthwhile reading. We know we are in a period of civilizational decay when such an amusing comment is in fact "news," as if we never thought of it before.

In a 1953 *Peanuts*, we see Lucy, absorbed in a book, walking by kids playing, shouting, "Hey, Lucy! C'mon and play in the pool."

She replies: "Nope, I'm reading."

Another girl invites her to jump rope. "Not now, I don't want to do anything but read my book."

She tells her friend, "This is the best book I've ever read." Sitting on the step, she continues, "It's called, 'The Three Little Kittens Who Lost Their Mittens' and it's all about these three kittens, see?" With her nose still in the book, Lucy explains to an increasingly annoyed little girl with a pony tail and a jump rope, "I've never read a book that I've enjoyed so much."

To which the girl logically inquires: "What other books have you read?"

Lucy, walking away, still with her eyes on the book, oblivious to the import of the question, replies, "This is the only one."[2]

They say the "man of one book" is dangerous. But I am with Lucy. You have to start somewhere. It is one of the blessings of life actually to enjoy the first book we ever read, as well, no doubt, as the last one.

Recently, a grand-nephew of mine, who is about to enter a public high school, showed me the school bulletin listing the classes offered in this rather large school. It was bewildering. There seemed to be as many courses offered at this high school as we have in most colleges. Whenever we see a school claiming to have a "core curriculum," moreover, with about seventy different ways of meeting the requirement, all mostly up to the student to select which ones to take, we know no real core curriculum exists.

Furthermore, we know that no real "core" curriculum exists when we cannot agree on what it ought to contain, or even whether

2   *The Complete Peanuts*, 1953.

it ought to exist. Thus, in practice, there ends up being many "core" curricula, take your choice. Each politically correct view has its input of what "ought" to be there, no one having any other criteria by which to include or exclude anything. The average core curriculum is closer to the Tower of Babel than any other known construct. The end result is that what was once considered something that everyone had to read to be at all aware of the nobility of our lives is not read by anyone or, if so, only in an adversarial context. Not only is Aristotle's *Ethics* itself "beyond good and evil," to steal a phrase from Nietzsche, but it is beyond comprehension in a world where all "values" are either equal or less than equal. If all "values" are equal, then nothing that is called "value" is of much importance.

II.

Recently, Magdalen Goffin gave me a copy of her new biography of her father, the English Catholic writer, E. I. Watkin.[3] It seems that one of her great-grandparents on her mother's side, from the early nineteenth century, was Herbert Ingram. He was the founder of the *Illustrated London News*, a major newspaper innovation of its time. Ingram is said to have formulated three "sure-fire" principles of how to run a successful journal: 1) "People enjoy reading about crimes and disasters"; 2) Papers with photos or pictures "sell more copies than those without," and 3) "Human beings of the poorer sort are exceedingly credulous especially when it comes to mattes of health."

These principles, when put together, I take it, mean that if we want to interest most people in reading and make money at the same time, the best way to do it is to produce an essay or text about some disaster, accompanied with graphic photos, preferably something related to health and its easy restoration, say with non-prescription pills. I would be hard pressed to say this formula still does not work like a charm and is repeated regularly in the daily

---

3   (*The Watkin Path*, Sussex Academic Press, 2006)

editions of almost any paper or television station any place in the world.

This useful information, however, does broach the question of reading in our education, especially about what was once known as "book learning." I am familiar with the notion of a paper-less world. In fact, almost everything today that appears on paper first is formulated and then preserved in an electronic environment. Paper is not where you begin to write, but where you end and not always then. After about ten years of e-mail, I no longer can calculate the number of good letters I have received which have ceased to exist because they were on ephemeral electronic format and not written by hand on paper. I sometimes wonder why someone has not yet written a printed book entitled, *My Favorite Deleted E-mails*.

Now, I know that it is almost impossible to eradicate something that once appears on-line. From comments of lawyers seeking to convict us, nothing we have ever put in electronic format ever disappears. Its permanence is the closest thing we have to immortality in the modern world. Still, we do not usually read whole books on-line unless we have to, and even if we have to, we usually first print them out. As far as I can tell, far from the computer eliminating paper, it is one of its primary generators, precisely both for ease of reading and for a kind of alternate permanence. The growers of trees and other paper pulp products must love the computer.

Besides, something about a book irradiates its own mystique. I continue to maintain that what we mean by education, that strange word, still has mostly to do with books, books we possess, keep. Recently, I was given yet another book, this time a friend of mine was in London, the same man that gave me Belloc's *Places*. He came across Maurice Baring's *Lost Lectures*. Somewhere he found a copy of this relatively rare book, a book published by Peter Davies in London, in 1932. The Preface to this book begins with the following sentence: "These *Lost Lectures* are for the most part talks delivered to imaginary audiences." What else does anyone need but this enticing invitation to make him hasten to join this "imaginary audience"!

John Paul I wrote a famous book called *Illustrissimi*. The book contained his never-delivered letters to famous people from Don Quixote to Chesterton. I rather like the idea of giving a talk to an imaginary audience or writing a letter to someone long dead to express my appreciation for what he wrote even if I came across it long after the author had died. Someone also gave me the review from the *New York Times* (May 5), replete with photos of author and book cover, of Peter Kelly's *The Book of Lost Books: An Incomplete History of Great Books You'll Never Read*. This title is not unlike a medical encyclopedia, with graphics, of diseases not yet known. But, as Herbert Ingram implied, who can resist reading about such terrible diseases?

After a certain age, one begins to suspect that the world is full of books that he will never read. One of my definitions of a noble life, well lived, is one in which, on the occasion of death, the man in question still has many books on his shelves not yet read. This is not to deny that we want to check also the ones that he did read. *Tell me what you read, and I will tell you what you are.* I believe the same principle would hold if we put it negatively, "Tell me what you don't read, and I will tell you what you are."

III.

But, as I intimated, it is not so much whether you are able to read, but what you read when you are able. The world is full of folks who can read but who, in fact, have read little or nothing. It is also full of folks who constantly read but reading nothing that is noble, nothing that really might move their souls. But to read well and accurately, we need the grammar, we need to know the parts of speech, how things fit together. This seems basic, even when spell-check and grammar-check are on our standard computer software.

However, a gentleman in Canada recently sent me an on-line review of a book called *The War against Grammar*, which review appeared in the *Bryn Mawr Classical Review* in 2003. He suspected that I would be astonished to read the following sentence: "Opposition to the teaching of grammar is now almost universal among professors of education and the 80,000 members of the NCTA (National Council of Teachers of English)." I was indeed astonished, but also I was delighted at the further comment of the review, Jeremiah Reedy. It seems that teachers of foreign languages find it difficult to teach when students do not know their English grammar. To keep their jobs, foreign language teachers resort to attracting students by using culture to replace grammar as a tool of learning. They study maps, menus, and monuments. Finally, the author of the book, David Mulroy, "took his son out of a public school and began home-schooling him when homework in French consisted of making a dessert of mangoes and powdered sugar, 'a favorite (dessert) in Francophone Africa!'"

So we must have what Dorothy Sayers once called the "tools" of learning, which she said, in a famous essay that can still be easily found on Google, were in fact "The Lost Tools of Learning." Still, as we think of graduating seniors, of whatever stripe, the most important thing that they can possess in their young souls is not just the "tools" of learning, but the desire, the *eros,* the love of learning. We see some of it already in Lucy reading her first book and ignoring every other distraction or temptation to do something else presumably more delightful, like swimming or jumping rope.

To all of us, there must come, as Plato said in the seventh book of the *Republic,* that awakening of our minds, minds we already have, that turning around, that astonishment that something exists that we do not know about but want to know. If our schools or universities conspire, by their theories or their atmosphere, to prevent us from wondering about the highest things, we are on our own. We need not be defeated by a very expensive education that teaches us that relativism is true, or by a free education that teaches things that corrupt us. I suppose what I want to say to students, at the end of any academic year, especially to those whom Plato called the "potential philosophers," not to be defeated either by one's own vices or one's own ideology or one's own lethargy. But this reaction can only happen to us if we suddenly are alerted by something outside of ourselves, something that is true or beautiful, something *that is.*

Fortunately, not a few passages can be found in our literature that serve to alert us, to wake us up. Let us imagine a young Lucy or the student taken out of the French class in which the making of a mango dessert was a substitute for learning grammar, but now grown to be twenty one or twenty two, still young. Their souls have now hopefully acquired some virtue, some grammar, some curiosity. To these, I would give as a graduation present the following famous passage from Boswell's *Journal of a Tour to the Hebrides with Samuel Johnson, LL.D.*

The day was Tuesday, October 19, 1768. That morning Boswell and Johnson breakfasted on the Island of Col. They took leave of "the young ladies, and of our excellent companion, Col, to whom we had been so much obliged." Finally they land on "that illustrious Island, which was once the luminary of the Caledonian regions, whence savage clans and roving barbarians derived their benefits of knowledge and the blessings of religion."

Johnson, in seeing this place, was much moved by the scene before him. Fortunately for us, Boswell was there to record what he said, which was as follows:

To abstract the mind from all local emotion would be impossible, if it were endeavoured, and would be foolish if it were possible. Whatever withdraws us from the power of our senses, whatever makes the past, the distant, or the future, predominate over the present, advances us in the dignity of thinking beings. Far from me, and from my friends, be such frigid philosophy as may conduct us indifferent and unmoved over any ground that has been dignified by wisdom, bravery or virtue. That man is little to be envied, whose patriotism would not gain force upon the plain of *Marathon*, or whose piety would not grow warmer among the ruins of *Iona*.

Should those graduating this year from whatever college, in whatever place, not know of the plains of Marathon or the ruins of Iona, they can assume they have lost much time in what is called their education.

In a footnote to this passage, Boswell adds: "Had our Tour produced nothing else but this *sublime passage*, the world must have
acknowledged that it was not made in vain. The present respectable
President of the Royal Society was so much struck on reading it,
that he clasped his hands together, and remained for some time in
an attitude of silent admiration." We can find much in local things.
If we have never stood before something that moved us to "silent
admiration," we have not begun our proper human lives.

Yet we can read without learning. Or we can have read only
one book that is the "greatest" one we have ever read. We can read
many things none of which move our souls to attend to *what is.*
Johnson was right. The man is "little to be envied" who can come
across great, pious, and noble things without their causing a ripple
of light in his soul. What makes education, such as it is, worthwhile
are precisely those defining moments of turning around, of being
struck by something that calls us out of ourselves, be it the crimes
and disasters recounted in the *London Illustrated News*, the *Lost
Lectures* of Maurice Baring, the "Lost Tools of Learning" of
Dorothy Sayers, the *Book of Lost Books* of Peter Kelly, or the plain
of Marathon and the ruins of Iona, where our patriotism should
"gain force" and our piety grow "warmer."

Chapter 9
WHAT MAKES LIBERAL EDUCATION "LIBERAL?"[*]

A man who has not been in Italy, is always conscious of an inferiority, from his not having seen what it is expected a man should see. The grand object of travelling is to see the shores of the Mediterranean. On those shores were the four great Empires of the world; the Assyrian, the Persian, the Grecian, and the Roman.—All our religion, almost all our law, almost all our arts, almost all that sets us above savages, has come to us from the shores of the Mediterranean.
— Samuel Johnson, Thursday, April 11, 1776.[1]

Every systematic science, the humblest and the noblest alike, seems to admit of two distinct kinds of proficiency; one of which may be properly called scientific knowledge of the subject, while the other is a kind of educational acquaintance with it. For an educated man should be able to form a fair off-hand judgment as to the goodness or badness of the method used by a professor in his exposition. To be educated is in fact to be able to do this; and even the man of universal education we deem to be such in virtue of his having this ability.
— Aristotle, *Parts of Animals*, (639a1–7).

I.

Presuming to speak about liberal education at a college like Christendom is perhaps rash, rather like bringing the proverbial coals to

---

[*] Lecture presented at Christendom College, Front Royal, Virginia, 2004.
1 *Boswell's Life of Johnson* (New York: Oxford, 1931), vol. II, pp. 24–25.

Newcastle. This school was founded with an articulated notion of a liberal education in its very conception. This education, taking advantage of the freedom of religion tradition and private initiative, included in a coherent relationship the theological and the philosophical traditions in all their fullness, with an added emphasis on the literary and artistic elements of the culture. I was actually here at the Front Royal campus when Bishop Thomas Welsh dedicated it in 1979. What was then, it seemed at the time, little more than a tenuous hope has become a visible and concrete reality with its own place, its own history, and its own way of going about learning both the practical and the higher things.

Sometimes, it seems, that only in small schools can one hope to learn something of everything. Larger universities often end up giving us, not "a little bit about a lot of things," as the old song went, but a lot about an enormous variety of the little things, none of which is ever put together in a sensible whole. Philosophy, we recall, is precisely the knowledge of the whole, something our minds seek of their very nature.

The question that I propose for consideration is, at first sight, straight-forward. "What makes a liberal education 'liberal'?" In recent years, I have taken to using the phrase "liberal learning" rather than "liberal education." One book of mine is entitled *Another Sort of Learning*, a second *Students' Guide to Liberal Learning*. Both of these books are addressed to those who are either going to college or who have finished formal education but who realize that they never learned much about what really counted in human life. Once someone knows how to read, remedies are always available for what we missed. But we have to want to know. We have to have a sense of unsettlement in our souls about the inadequacy of what we have learned, even in the best or most famous schools. For the comfortably contented, there probably is no salvation, intellectual or otherwise.

The reason I prefer the word "learning" has to do, in part, with a remark of Chesterton who pointed out that the word "education," by itself, does not refer to any subject matter. It does not describe what it is that we ought to know. Rather the noun education derives from the Latin verb, *educere*. It means to lead forth. It refers to the process of bringing forth, the process of learning. The process in itself is not an independent topic apart from what is to be known and how what is known falls into some order of things. Thus, a doctorate in "education" would not necessarily indicate our knowing anything at all except various methodologies. Studying "education" is not studying that which makes us educated. Knowing what education is includes the living of it. It is rather like Aristotle's virtue, knowing what virtue is does not indicate whether we are virtuous or not. We are both to know what virtue or education is and to practice it.

Samuel Johnson, in his above-cited remarks on travel, tells us that we go to Mediterranean shores because things worth knowing were begun and flourished there. We can, to be sure, learn something by traveling to Antarctica, or to the Moon. But of religion, law, the arts, we will learn far more about everything in this rather small part of the world. What sets us apart from the savages is what we know and how we live based on what we know. And one of the things we learn, as Aristotle again tells us, is that man himself can be, if he chooses, much worse than the savages or the beasts. But when it comes to learning and travel, I see that Christendom has a summer program that sets down in Burgundy, still within the reaches of the Mediterranean. Today almost every American university has some sort of program somewhere around the shores of this inland sea. Yet, it does not seem to be enough to save us and we wonder why.

To be educated, Aristotle tells us, to wherever we travel, we should be able to form some considered judgment on what we see, on what the specialists tell us about their methods and what they conclude. We are not to be overwhelmed or baffled by esoteric statistics or sophisticated arguments in foreign languages. We should realize that there is such a thing as universal culture, something that has been with us at least since Plato. The educated man is not only the man who knows science but the man who can judge its validity and where it fits among the other things that are likewise known. Far be it from Aristotle to minimize the worth of scientific knowledge, but he did recognize its limits. He understood that it must itself be seen in a broader context that requires something more than itself to judge rightly about its meaning.

II.

In the fourth book of Aristotle's *Ethics,* we find a virtue called *elutheria,* often translated as liberality or generosity. This virtue, along with its parallel, munificence, has had enormous influence on our civilization. This virtue relates to our ruling our own property and wealth, whether we have little or much. Let me approach this virtue of liberality, as it relates to education, through James Hitchcock's book, *The Supreme Court and Religion.* Hitchcock points out that most of the Court cases dealing with religion make it to the Court's docket because of some issue involving property rights, some bequest, some inheritance, some purchase or sale of land. This very fact suggests that all religion has some tangible effect in the world, but that civil authorities are limited in their dealings with it to these effects. We want religions to be free to define themselves without the state, though perhaps not without the natural law.

Hitchcock cited the 1914 case, decided by Justice Charles Evans Hughes, of a Benedictine monk by the name of Wirth. He had been a religious for fifty years with a vow of poverty. He belonged to a monastery in New Jersey but died in Minnesota, presumably outside the Order. Wirth was a writer who made a certain amount of money in royalties during his lifetime. When he died in 1904, the administrator of his estate claimed these royalties as Wirth's private property. Therefore, they belonging to the estate, not to the Benedictines. The Court, however, ruled in favor of the Benedictines. The man had a vow of poverty that forbad him to own property privately. The executor of Wirth's estate claimed that this vow was "a violation of freedom to forbid monks to hold property." But Hughes, for the Court, argued that Wirth freely repudiated this right of ownership and assigned any subsequent personal income to the Order. Besides, Hughes wryly added, the value of Wirth's writings probably had much to do with his Benedictine status.[2]

Now, I cite this case in the context of Aristotle's virtue of liberality for two reasons. First, in the case of a monk, though he need not, he is free to give up his right to property and income to some communal religious organization if he chooses. The right is "alienable." In the monastic tradition, it was understood that this giving up one's right to private property resulted in the monk's liberty or freedom from the obligations inherent in property ownership. The vow was designed to free him, not limit him.[3] "Free him for what?" has always been a basic consideration, be it in religion, education, or politics. The monk thus could, with the protection of the law, follow the Gospel principle whereby a man sold his possessions, gave them to the poor, and followed the Lord.

Greek thought also had this sense of the philosopher's not being encumbered with cares caused by property. Socrates prided himself in being a poor man who, unlike the sophists, took no fees for what he taught. We must remember, to be sure, that Socrates' chosen poverty was not without some inconvenience to his wife, Xantippe, and their three boys. This factor may well be why the vow of chastity, in the Christian tradition, was also related to the vow of poverty. Freedom to philosophize, in any case, implies freedom from undue attachment to property and wealth. The vow or practice of poverty also intimated that there were things higher than wealth. As such, it did not, in principle, deny that wealth had its necessary place.

On the other hand, the virtue of liberality was itself based precisely on private ownership and its worthwhileness. We really owned what we could use or give away. This is a point Aristotle made evident in the second book of the *Politics* over against Plato's communality of property, wives, and children described in the

---

2   James Hitchcock, *The Supreme Court and Religion in American Life* (Princeton: Princeton University Press, 2004), vol. I, pp. 32–33.
3   See James V. Schall, "The Christian Guardians," *The Politics of Heaven and Hell* (Lanham, MD.: University Press of America, 1984), pp. 67–82.

famous fifth book of the *Republic*. The virtue of liberality meant that one showed how he ruled himself by using his property or wealth for some normal or noble purpose. One's property did not determine someone to its demands but allowed him to use it for some definite purpose, basically for our material well-being.

The virtue of liberality showed that a man was "free" to do what he wanted because he owned property, which in itself is a good. Aristotle in fact recognized that property enabled us freely to benefit others because we had the wherewithal to do so. But more importantly, liberality meant that we ruled ourselves so that we were not determined by our property. The judgment of our character depended upon whether we showed ourselves free to do this ruling of our property by actually doing it for a purpose apart from selfishness or stinginess.

In the case of munificence, that is, in case we have large amounts of property or wealth, the worthy person used this wealth for a noble purpose. He might endow the good, say, hospitals, or the true, say, universities, or the beautiful, say, museums. He did not just hoard his wealth, or just keep it. Wealth brings into being and sustains higher purposes because of the wealthy man's rule of his own soul and his sensitiveness to what is noble among men within the polity. In this way, wealth itself was subsumed into a higher purpose, even apart from state bureaucracy. The relation between individual virtue and culture is thus very close.

In both of these cases, when we give up wealth voluntarily or when we use it for a good or noble purpose, we are "free." We do not become "slaves" of what we own. I might add, that Aristotle does not think that people with ordinary wealth are any worse off than those with great wealth simply because of more or less material goods. The virtue depends not on how much we have but on what we do with what we do have. Aristotle is able to see nobility in endowing a university, or in giving a cup of water, or in offering a glass of wine to a friend. The poor, in this sense, are not deprived of any real opportunity to practice virtue simply because they are poor. The greatest examples of liberality may well be found among the poor and the less well-off, but among those who have more too.

A slave, on the other hand, is someone who is precisely not free, not *causa sui*, either legally or because he cannot objectively control himself, a drug addict, for instance. The long history of slavery and freedom does have something to do with this question of liberality because slavers were considered at one time to be property. Real freedom required something more than legality. It is possible to argue that, from the viewpoint of willingness and ability to attend the higher things, we can have legally free societies yet still full of "slaves" who never really come to terms with the things most worth knowing. One must be careful how he states that point.

As Allan Bloom suggested in the *Closing of the American Mind*, it may be possible to have universities full of students and professors who, in Aristotle's terms, are none the less "slaves." That is, they are imprisoned by their own desires and decisions. They lacked true knowledge about what things are or else they lack enough virtue to find out. And at another level, we must admit that even St. Paul thought that slaves could save their souls without being politically free. There are saints who were slaves, just as there are probably academics who have lost their souls.

III.

My topic is "What is 'liberal' about liberal education?" As we have seen in the case of the virtue of liberality, "liberal" may mean that we are sufficiently self-controlled that we will not let our wealth interfere with our responsibilities to accomplish or to know worthy things. Rather, we will use it as an opportunity to fulfill the other virtues, including the notions of benevolence or charity, whereby we are also free to give away what we possess. The capacity freely to give something away may be close to the highest thing we can do, including, in a sense, the giving of ourselves. But the most precious things we possess are not our material goods, valuable a they are.

A Chinese lady I know remarked that "You cannot do anything without money." Within obvious limits, this is true. But there are many things that we cannot do with money, which, I believe, was the main point of Dickens' *Christmas Carol*. It was also Aristotle's reason for not giving money as the definition of happiness in the first book of the *Ethics*, though it might easily be confused for it since it seems that honor, pleasure, and even knowledge could be purchased with it.

In his book, *A General Theory of Authority*, Yves Simon has a remarkable sub-section entitled, "Freedom from the Self." Here, Simon brings up the question of why a vow or a promise is a great freedom. Chesterton, in his essay, "In Defence of Rash Vows," had said that the only freedom worth having is the freedom to bind ourselves, as in marriage.[4] In this sense, to be "liberal" is to be bound. Simon brings up this same point. We want a "mastery over desire such that, for the sake of a law, for the sake of the good, for the sake of God, a man be free to choose, if he pleases, and without a struggle against overwhelming difficulties, the dignity and the exclusive dedication of indissoluble marriage."[5] This view of freedom is seen over against the view that freedom means not being bound to anything, including the beloved. Freedom, in this latter sense, means "autonomy" wherein nothing can bind anything to anything as there is no law but what we give ourselves.

I dwell on these ideas here because they are the ones, in other areas, that have undermined any notion of a content to "liberal" education. Simon states the issue well:

> These expressions "free love," "free union," are dishonestly loaded with the philosophy which interprets freedom as spontaneity, and preferably as the spontaneity of animal desires. If, on the contrary, freedom is understood to be an uppermost kind of active indifference and mastery, whoever finds "free love" and "free union" good enough for him is but one who has chosen not to exercise

4   G. K. Chesterton, "In Defence of Rash Vows," *The Defendant* (New York: Dodd, Mead, 1914), pp. 18–26.
5   Yves Simon, *A General Theory of Authority* (Notre Dame: University of Notre Dame Press, 1980), pp. 149–50.

mastery over the lower impulses of his nature. That love is most truly an act of freedom which is strong enough to stay alive and remain in control when sensuous desires have become inert or have changed their way.[6]

From this angle, then, the term "liberal" will mean a freedom to bind oneself against those inner forces that would deflect us from ever being obliged to know the truth or follow it, choose it, once we have discovered it.

IV.

What is "liberal" about liberal education? In November, 1954, on a very black night, Lucy and Charlie Brown are looking into the night sky. Lucy asks, "Charlie Brown, what would you do if the Moon fell right on your head?"

The two are next silhouetted against a light. Charlie is, cautious, puzzled. "What do you mean, what would I do?"

And Lucy responds, "Just what I said, what would you do?"

Lucy continues to look into the night sky, but Charlie responds truthfully, "I haven't got the slightest idea."

Finally, Lucy calmly turns to a deflated Charlie to ask him, "How come you never think about things like that?"[7]

Liberal education clearly has to do with what we think about. It is about taste and emotions certainly, but these too need thinking about. We might say that liberal education exists in order that we might think about the important things, things we never thought of or thought clearly of by ourselves. But this emphasis on the highest things should not unduly prejudice us from noticing the little things, the things that may not count for much, but of which much of human life consists. What indeed would we do "if the Moon fell on our heads"? This question is amusing because it is absurd. And it is because of its absurdity that we can laugh at it. We laugh

6   Ibid., p. 150.
7   *The Complete Peanuts* (Seattle: Fantagraphic, 2004), p. 288.

because we understand incongruities, things that look like they fit together but do not, or things that do not seem to fit together but do. But the very silliness of the question serves to remind us that there are things we ought to think about, things for which we might well be blamed for never asking or thinking about them ourselves. A liberal education, after all, can ultimately be found only in our own souls. It does not exist apart from them.

How are we to learn if no one ever tells us, if no one ever teaches us? To be sure, we are not totally helpless by ourselves. Our minds are themselves active powers, open to *what is*. And what is it to be taught other than to be guided more easily, more efficiently so that we ourselves, with our own powers, can see something that others have already seen? Aquinas' famous expression, *contemplata tradere*, means that it is a better thing to pass on what we have contemplated than merely to contemplate it by ourselves. The expression reminds us that there is a certain inner urgency in *what is*, almost as if things are designed both *to be* and to be known. Somehow, we are not "free" if we keep what is true to ourselves, even if it is ours and indeed intended for ourselves.

Political and social efforts to prevent truth from being known, or even discussed in the name of truth, are widespread, perhaps more so today than ever before. A liberal age is loathe to admit this illiberality but, as we shall suggest in a moment, there is a theoretic reason for this denial. Nor do I mean that we should become intellectual pests constantly bothering others with our latest ideas. Still, philosophy exists ultimately in conversation, the highest act of friendship, as Aristotle told us.

What does this import for the "liberal" side of a liberal education? It means, I think, that the burden of finding the truth of things, of finding what does in fact make us free, may often require us to find it in channels other than those wherein we would expect to find it. Plato's "Academy," it seems, was set up precisely, as Eric Voegelin tells us,[8] as a place in which truth could be pursued when Athens rejected a more public way in its official execution of

8   Eric Voegelin, *Plato* (Baton Rouge: Louisiana State University Press), p. 6.

Socrates. Our modern experience is that truth may not be safe either in the democracy or in the academy.

Ultimately, I think, what is "liberal" about liberal education is the awareness that our minds are measured by reality. Truth is, as Aquinas said, the conformity of mind with *what is*. It is true that in moral, political, and artistic things, in their own way, things can be otherwise. That is their nature. To be aware of this variability is essential to the freedom and the truth inherent in practical things. Not all houses have to look alike. Not every act of courage will be the same. In fact, no two acts will be exactly be the same, ever. There are many ways to construct any political regime without denying its essence.

But behind practical intellect always lies theoretical intellect. We live in an era, however, in which mind has declared its freedom from things. The autonomous man is the man who claims a freedom based on the premise that there are no binding norms or measures to be found in things. Things are devoid of forms. We "create" the only norms there are. We do not discover them. We are "free" to establish our own nature, our own definitions of good and evil.

This position has its own intellectual history, of course. But it essentially means there is nothing that binds the intellect, not even the principle of contradiction. Anything that seems mandatory is to be rejected as "alien." Human autonomy means that nothing exists but what is freely put there by human craft. No natural law or order can be found in things. Yves Simon, again, has, I think, spelled out the real issue:

> Even the first principles have become objects of free belief . . . . It cannot be said that this most radical interpretation of intellectual freedom belongs to the essence of liberalism. To be sure, a true liberal may confess that the principle of non-contradiction does not in any way depend upon the dispositions of our freedom. Only a few extremists openly hold the theory of a free adherence to the first principles. Yet the influence of this theory has not been negligible . . . . Though professed by few

persons, the theory of a free dominion over obviousness (contradiction) itself has been haunting the liberal movement after the fashion of a ghost . . . .[9]

This "ghost," I think, is no longer quite so invisible as in Simon's time over a half century ago.

The notion that the mind thinks as it wants, not as it must according to rules of logic and evidence, is what relates this version of liberalism to the basic theological view of Islam about Allah, namely the primacy of will, something that gets into western though through Occam and Hobbes. What does this notion of a will based philosophy have to do with liberal education? In the case of Islam, the only way to escape a completely arbitrary world is through revelation, through a complete, unquestioned obedience to the Koran, whatever it says, whatever the evidence of its own validity.

In the West, the term "liberal" in liberal education must begin with the notion that the freedom of the intellect is precisely its affirmation of *what is* and the principles of being that follow from it. Freedom is not a power to make things, including ourselves, to be otherwise, to restructure the state, the family, the inner soul. Rather it is the liberty to affirm and follow what we are wherein what we are is not something we make or define, but what we discover ourselves to be. It is, in short, the affirmation that we do not cause our own *to be*.

In conclusion, then, let me recall what I have tried to say. 1) "All our religion, almost all our law, almost all our arts, almost all that sets us above savages, has come to us from the shores of the Mediterranean." 2) "For an educated man should be able to form a fair off-hand judgment as to the goodness or badness of the method used by a professor in his exposition." 3) Studying education is not what makes us educated. 4) The vow of poverty is not a violation of freedom. 5) Liberality is the proper rule of our wealth so that we are free to use it as we ought. 6) "Whoever finds 'free

9   Simon, ibid., pp. 102–03.

love' and 'free union' good enough for him is but one who has chosen not to exercise mastery over the lower impulses of his nature." 7) Philosophy exists ultimately in conversation, the highest act of friendship. 8) "The theory of a free dominion over obviousness itself has been haunting the liberal movement after the fashion of a ghost." 9) What indeed "would you do if the Moon fell on your head"?

We are to be neither "savages," who live by instinct or emotion, nor "ghosts," who find no structure even to ourselves. One is tempted to say that the Moon has already fallen on our heads and we did not notice. The ultimate purpose of what is "liberal" in a liberal education is that we be free to acknowledge, because we have both virtue and mind, even what is obvious when no one else sees it or, worse, admits to seeing it.

Chapter 10

AQUINAS AND THE LIFE OF THE MIND[*]

*Sicut natura non deficit homini in necessariis, quamvis
non dederit sibi arma et tegumenta sicut aliis animanibus,
quia dedit ei raionem et manus, quibus possit haec sibi
acquirere; ita nec deficit homini in necessariis, quamvis
non daret sibi aliquod principum quo posset beatitudinem
consequi; hoc enim erat impossibile. Sed dedit ei liberum
arbitrium, qua possit converti ad Deum, qui eum faceret
beatum. 'Quae enim per amicos possumus, per nos
aliquliter possumus,' ut dicitur in III Eth. (1112b27).*
— Thomas Aquinas, *Summa Theologiae*, I–II, 5, 5, ad 1.[1]

That *strangeness* of things, which is the light in all poetry,
and indeed in all art, is really connected with their otherness; or what is called their objectivity. What is subjective
must be stale; it is exactly what is objective that is in this
imaginative manner strange. In this the great contemplative is the complete contrary of that false contemplative,
the mystic who looks only into his own soul, the selfish

---

[*] Lecture originally given at Ohio Dominican University, Columbus, Ohio,
2005, published by *New Blackfriars*, July, 2006.

[1] "Just as nature is not depriving anything to man in necessary things, although
she did not give him arms and hides as in other animals, because she gave
him reason and hands, by which he can acquire these things for himself; so
also neither is nature lacking to man in necessary things even though she did
not give him any principle by which he would be able to obtain beatitude,
for this was impossible. But she did give him free choice, by which he could
turn to God, who would make him happy. 'For those things that are through
friends, are equally through ourselves,' as Aristotle says in the Third Book of
his *Ethics*."

artist who shrinks from the world and lives only in his own mind. According to St. Thomas, the mind acts freely of itself, but its freedom exactly consists in finding a way out to liberty and the light of day; to reality and the land of the living.

— G. K. Chesterton, *St. Thomas Aquinas*, 1933.[2]

I.

Several winters ago, on the Feast of Thomas Aquinas, I had the pleasure of addressing a colloquium on this great saint at the University of St. Thomas at Fredericton, New Brunswick, in Canada.[3] Likewise, it is a delight and an honor this winter, on the Feast of St. Thomas, to be here at Ohio Dominican University in Columbus. I had actually been on this campus some quarter of a century ago. By chance, I had known Sister Camilla Mullay, O. P., who was engaged in writing a history of this college before she died not too long ago.

The history of a college is the memory of a college. What a college remembers, just as what we ourselves remember, pretty much defines what we are, what we choose to stand for, what we choose to reject or ignore. Among the principal things any college with the name "Dominican" in its title must, above all, remember is Thomas Aquinas. He was a man who seems to have remembered everything he ever read and who, subsequently, thought about everything he remembered. Indeed, he wrote about the very power of memory and its relation to thought. Aquinas knew more than he read. He also thought of a number of things no one before or after him has thought about or thought about quite so well. Yet, Thomas is most famous for his defense of ordinary things along with our natural ability to know them and to speak in our words

2   G. K. Chesterton, *St. Thomas Aquinas* (Garden City, N. Y.: Doubleday Image, 1956), pp. 183–84.
3   James V. Schall, "Aquinas and the Defense of Ordinary Things: On 'What Common Men Call Common Sense,'" *Fellowship of Catholic Scholars' Quarterly* 27 (Winter, 2004), pp. 16–22.

to indicate *what they are*. We can and do, like Adam, name things, whereby we can communicate with one another about the reality that surrounds us, the reality within us. Thomas Aquinas was a unique saint.

Aquinas was, as I like to recall, the only saint who was canonized merely for "thinking," as Cardinal von Schönborn once remarked of him. But this theme of "thinking" is what I want to speak to you about this morning. Why would "thinking" qualify for sanctity? Don't we "think" all the time? What, after all, is so unusual about thinking? And yet, we have intimations that thinking somehow brings us to the heart of things when we hear that Aristotle, who plays such a central role in Aquinas' life, defines his First Mover, or God, as "thought thinking on itself," a definition that Thomas himself will respect and develop once he knows of the revelation of the Trinity, of the inner life of the Godhead. That the second person of the Trinity was called, in revelation, "the Word" would not, I suspect, have overly surprised Aristotle. It was certainly intelligible to Aquinas.

And yet, Thomas is always very careful in speaking about what we can and cannot know about God. "It is impossible," he tells us, "through natural reason to come to a knowledge of the Trinity of Persons."[4] At first sight, we might think this an undue restriction. It looks to be a lowering to its own limits of our power of reasoning, of which we are quite proud. But Thomas adds that those who try to prove this doctrine by reason actually "denigrate" the faith by making its teaching simply circumscribed by the reaches of our own intellects and their mode of knowing. To claim that we can fully explain God by our own powers is, implicitly, a claim that we are God, which with any insight into ourselves, we are quite sure we are not. Still, it is all right to be what we are, individual human beings, not everything, not nothing, but something.

Nevertheless, Aquinas tells us that we can use our intellects to show that this central teaching about the inner Trinitarian life of God "is not impossible." We can show that the arguments against

4   I, 32, 1.

it are themselves contradictory, a principle that leads us to suspect that reason and revelation are not unrelated to each other. Indeed, because of the relations and processions within this inner life of God, Thomas concludes that God did not produce creatures because of any lack in the Godhead, as if He needed them for His own perfection or companionship. If He did "need" creation, He would be a very limited God. Rather He produced creatures, including ourselves, through a "love out of His own goodness."[5] We do not exist because of some lack or loneliness in God but because of His abundance. This fact makes our existence more, not less, glorious.

On the surface, Thomas Aquinas lived a rather short, even uneventful life. He was dead by the time he was forty-nine. He published his first treatises when he was in his early twenties. He was still working on the famous *Summa Theologiae* when he died. He completed only up to Book 3, chapter 6, of his Commentary on Aristotle's *Politics*. He did happily finish the commentaries on the *Ethics* and the *Metaphysics*. A commentary, incidentally, is a precise rendering of the text at hand so that its complete argument is presented in an orderly fashion. To be able to understand and explain a text, as it stands, not as we would like it to stand, must be the beginning of any true education.

It was said, moreover, that Aquinas could dictate three different books to his secretaries at the same time, a feat I do not recommend even with a computer, which he did not have. I have often wondered whether Aquinas could have written more than he did with a quill if he had the latest model Dell computer. I actually doubt it. It is difficult to see how he could have done more than he did in the relatively few years given to him. It is always worth one's effort to go to the library, locate them, and simply look at the *Opera Omnia* of Thomas Aquinas, to page through some of its many volumes just to have a sense of what he had written, of its scope and variety.

Augustine lived some thirty years longer than Aquinas, but wrote at least as much. Yet, it is said of Augustine that any one

5   I, 32, 1, ad 3.

who claims that he has read all Augustine's massive works is a liar. While you are at it, it is equally worthwhile to take a look at the *Opera Omnia* of Augustine, whom Aquinas cites more than any other author besides Scripture. And of Aquinas, whose *Summa Theologiae* alone reaches over 4,000 folio pages, it is said that if, when you are twenty-two, you start merely to read the corpus of Aquinas' work, and read diligently every day for eight hours, you probably could not have read, let alone comprehended or written, what Aquinas wrote by the time you are forty-nine, the age at which he died.

But my intention here is not to frighten you away from reading Aquinas because of the vastness of his output. Rather it is to indicate why it is not only possible to read him, but delightful, moving. There is no intellectual pleasure, I think, quite like reading and understanding even one article in the works of Thomas Aquinas. To learn to do so is worth your whole college career. Not to know him, I suspect, is equivalent to being educated in something but not precisely in everything, in the parts but not the whole. Indeed, not learning to read Aquinas is to deprive ourselves of the shortest and most concise avenue to those truths for which alone our minds were created in the first place.

Aquinas did live in some interesting places, places which we can still visit, in fact. He was born across from the great Abbey of Monte Cassino, between Rome and Naples. Early on, he was a student at the Abbey. Later, after joining the Dominicans, he was in Paris, in Cologne, in Orvieto, Rome, and Naples. He died in a beautiful Cistercian Abbey called Fossanova, on his way to a Council of the Church. In those years, I believe, the Dominican friars had a rule that their members, on going from place to place, had to walk. I believe Albertus Magnus, Aquinas' great teacher, was nick-named something like "boots," because of this tradition. One hesitates to call this rule "inspired," but it is indeed a good way to see Europe, or any place else, namely on foot. Indeed, in some sense, you don't see a place until, as it were, you "see" it on foot, particularly, I suspect, places like Paris, Cologne, Orvieto, Naples, and certainly Rome.

Thomas was said to be quite a large man, at least the size of a tackle on the Buckeyes. Still, the walking everywhere probably was not formally designed to keep the thirteenth century Dominicans in shape, though it may have had, *per accidens*, as Thomas would say, that happy effect which we moderns build so many gyms and exercise machines to achieve in lieu of walking. The alternative in the thirteenth century to going to Paris from Naples on foot was not on the airbus, or the *"rapido"* train on the European railroads, or a comfortable Mercedes-Benz sedan, but a donkey or horse. Such animal transport could make the trip faster, no doubt, than walking, whether more comfortably, I leave to your imagination.

II.

In the first passage I cited in the beginning, we note that nature gave us "reason and hands" instead of more substantial claws or hides with which to fight or protect ourselves. Notice it is assumed that we, like the animals, may need to do precisely this, defend ourselves. In a definition of man going back to his philosophic master, Aristotle, man is said to be that being in the universe that alone has this combination of mind and hands. Without mind, hands would be merely claws or flippers; but without hands, minds could not get out of themselves into the world to make or do anything. It is a shrewd, vivid definition. The purpose of claws and hides in animals is to defend, protect, and provide for themselves. Human beings can figure out how to do this very thing even better by the use of their reason and hands.

Already here we have an instance of God expecting us to do things for ourselves. We might call it the philosophic basis of entrepreneurship, of economics, even. The world would not be more perfect, contrary to what we might at first think, if everything were done for us. Notice also that in this passage Aquinas is answering an implied objection of great force and influence. Somehow, the objection reads, whatever caused man to be the kind of being he is, God let us say, did not give him what he needed, what was necessary, to accomplish his purpose in the world. Clearly this claim is an attack on the creator. He did not give us what we needed to accomplish our purpose. He was inadequate, unjust, and niggardly. Thus, since we are deprived of what we need, nothing is our fault.

Even worse, the accusation proceeds, besides not having claws or hides, God did not give us any principle by which we could easily achieve complete happiness by our own powers. It is in a passage like this where Aquinas is most succinct, most amazing. First he makes the totally laconic remark that it would be "impossible" for God to do this. The kind of happiness for which we are created is quite beyond our natural powers to give. In other words, we are given more than we deserve. Are we therefore to despair because we do not have this principle under our own control? Not at all. Why not? Because, Aquinas states, we have been given a power of free choice by which we can turn to God. We are not, in other words, as lacking as we might at first think.

Why does that solve the problem of why we are not given, in necessary things, that is, in the most necessary things, a principle of our happiness? To answer, Aquinas simply makes a brief citation from Aristotle's treatment of friendship in the *Ethics*. If a friend does something for us or we for him, we can consider that it is done by and for us. The possibility of this happening has to do with the Incarnation, in which Christ said, in John's Last Supper, that He no longer considers us servants but friends. Thus, nature is not incomplete because something is lacking to us. From these seminal passages we can conclude both that there are things we must do for ourselves and things we must receive from our friends, including divine ones. And since we are free, we must choose to receive them as we choose to accept what our friends do for us. Who else, I ask you, but Aquinas tells us these things so briefly, so insightfully?

Let us now take a look at the second citation, the one from Chesterton's biography of Aquinas. This wonderful book of Chesterton has caused many a good philosopher to despair. How could an English journalist like Chesterton, with no apparent academic learning, who seems to have skimmed over a few books on Aquinas and looked at perhaps the *Summa*, have ever managed to tell us what Aquinas was about? Yet, few books do it better. Indeed, later on, I will mention a couple of books on Aquinas that might help you to get started in discovering him. In fact, I will mention them here. They are, besides the Chesterton book, two books of Josef Pieper, *A Guide to Thomas Aquinas* and the *Silence of St. Thomas*, any book on Aquinas by Ralph McInerny, A. D. Sertillanges, *The Intellectual Life*, and Peter Kreeft's *Summa of the Summa*.

Chesterton begins by pointing out the fact that things in reality are "strange," as he calls them. He calls this "strangeness" the "light of all poetry." What does he mean? He means that the reality, the being, of what is not ourselves is simply there to be discovered. What we find is not some Cartesian projection of our inner mind onto things. Things are received into our minds, but after our manner of knowing them. Our minds are capable of receiving *what is*, into ourselves, into our minds. By simply being ourselves, we are in our proper knowing, what is not ourselves. We are concerned with the "otherness" of things, with the fact that they are simply out there and we can know them. Chesterton next compares the true contemplative who beholds *what is* with the "mystic who looks only into his own soul, or the selfish artist who shrinks from the world and lives only in his own mind."

This latter is a sentence full of blunt philosophic controversy. It is true that we ourselves also are created things. Our self-reflection reaches to our awareness that we are not the ground of our own being. Our own minds are not complete if they only know themselves and not what is not ourselves. Chesterton adds, marvelously, that our minds are made to "act freely." But this freedom does not mean that we, in our freedom, create the world, as so much of modernity in its autonomy holds. Rather it means that we are free to direct ourselves to *what is*, but we are not determined to do so. We are to use our liberty to get out of ourselves to see what is there, to wonder about what it is that is not ourselves. This is how Chesterton used the word "strangeness" to emphasize that what we encounter is never what we could have previously imagined by our own powers.

III.

In a Christmas letter I received from a doctor in Mt. Vernon, Ohio, I noticed that on the left hand border of his letter, he had placed a photograph of Thomas Aquinas. Underneath this photo are the following words from Aquinas: "The greatest good that one can do to his neighbor is lead him to the truth." I despair of finding the exact source of this citation in St. Thomas. I confess looking through the questions in the *Summa* on truth. However, it does not matter. This is certainly St. Thomas. It is something that I want to comment on since truth is the purpose of thinking. Thinking for thinking's sake without a measure or standard that tells us whether a thought is true or not is simply a kind of vapid chaos of thoughts too fuzzy to manifest any order.

Today, no doubt, this emphasis on truth is an absolutely counter-cultural position. Truth is said to be our "enemy." Its claims divide us. Its very existence is a sign of "fanaticism." The truth will not make us free. No, our freedom makes the truth. Chesterton had it quite wrong. Freedom, it is said, is not limited and measured by *what is*. So understood, of course, truth makes no claim on us. We need not take it into consideration in our doing what we do, whatever we do. We insist on being "accepted," not "judged."

Yet, we have Aquinas here telling us that the greatest service we can give to our neighbor is to lead him to the truth. Is it not giving him a cup of water? The two activities are not contradictory, of course. Still before we can give anyone a cup of water, we have to know what water is. We have to know that the water we give is drinkable, not poisonous. We have to know the "truth," in other words, about water. And we have to act on this truth lest we be not free.

Now Aquinas was quite insightful when it came to the question of how to "lead" someone to the truth. The *Summa* itself was written precisely for beginners. Aquinas was a common sense and a common man philosopher. While he discussed almost every topic imaginable, he had the marvelous facility of breaking the matter up into human-sized "bites," as it were. He wrote so that the reader could understand, step by step. This is why, in Aquinas, one can find some of his most remarkable insights in brief, two or three sentence answers to objections. In reading Aquinas, we always have to be ready to be overwhelmed by something we never thought of. Josef Pieper's books are full of these brief, deeply penetrating citations from Aquinas. I think especially of his book, *The Truth of All Things*.

Let me take, for instance, this concise answer to an objection to a question entitled, "*Utrum Veritas Sit Pars Justitiae.*" The objection stated that "justice is to render another what is due," the classical definition of justice. But if we give "truth" to someone, it does not seem like a true "debt," like owing money. Therefore, the objection concludes, truth is not a part of justice.

Here is how Aquinas went about answering this objection. First, he recalled that man is a "social animal." That is, he must live in society and in the polity, as Aristotle had said. It is natural for him to do so. But a human being owes to another that which is necessary to live in society. Obviously, men cannot live with each other in society unless they "trust one another in manifesting the truth to one another." The fact that someone speaks what is true "does not seem other than to render a debt to him."[6] In other words, telling the truth and trusting in words spoken are the bases of our living together and therefore what we "owe" to one another.

Aquinas, as I intimated, seems at first sight to differ in emphasis from Plato who was very dubious of words themselves, especially written words. We recall, of course, that the "disputation," the primary form of discourse in the middle ages, was itself oral. Issues of honesty, integrity, logic, and will are usually much more visible in oral argument than in the written word. But Aquinas did not look on the admitted "strangeness" in things as something that hindered him from any attempt to explain them. Quite the opposite, the whole structure of Aquinas' work was presupposed to the proposition that it is possible to make things clear and to know, at

6   II–II, 109, 3, ad 1.

the least outlines, of what could not be known. Aquinas is a philosopher of light not of hiddenness. Yet, he does not ever doubt that there are things beyond the human intellect's power to know. With Aristotle, he thinks that knowing as much as we can about divine things is the highest task that we can be about. He thinks in fact that the desire to know the truth of things, and indeed finally to know them after the manner of our limited being, is why we exist in the first place.

Thomas Aquinas is a man who spent his life thinking. The purpose of thinking is to know the truth of *what is*. We do not make what is not ourselves. Thus, we find in reality a strangeness and a brightness, a wonder about what is there and why it is there. We can act freely only if we know the truth. We do not will truth to be truth, but we find it there as if it has in itself some being, some order. We affirm *what is*. But we can choose not to know the truth, though it is not possible to act unless there is some shred of truth left in what we hold. We can and should, moreover, know what is not true. Facing the truth of things is both our glory and out burden.

In an old *Peanuts* series from November, 1952, Lucy and Charlie Brown are playing marbles. In the first series, Lucy yells happily "I won again, I won again!" The reason she won she tells Charley is because of his last "stupid play." She adds yet again, "I won again!" And she asks Charlie, "Aren't you happy for me?"

In the next sequence, the winning continues, she tells Charlie that she has beaten him "three thousand times."

Charlie is embarrassed and says "rats."

Lucy naturally accuses him of being a poor loser.

But at last, in the final sequence, Charlie wins a game. He can hardly believe it. He throws up his arms and says, "I've never been so happy in all my life."

But Lucy tells him, "I just let you win because I really felt sorry for you." This completely deflates Charlie, but Lucy consoles him, "It's always better to know the truth."[7]

7   *The Complete Peanuts, 1950–52* (Fantagraphics Books, 2004).

But the fact is, that it is indeed, as Lucy says, "always better to know the truth." And why, in conclusion, is it so difficult to know the truth? In part, it is because our lives are not in order so that we cannot bear the truth because we know that it requires us to change our lives. So, to cover ourselves, we create our own truths. But another reason is that we do not go about studying for the truth in the right way. St. Thomas was aware of both of these problems. But on this occasion, let me say some final words about why we might find learning the important things so difficult.

The *Summa Theologiae* of Thomas Aquinas is famous for being directed to beginners, not for the already learned as were his other works like his *Quaestiones Disputatae*. At the very beginning of the *Summa*, Aquinas has three brief bits of advice for students who are confused and overwhelmed by the difficulties of knowing, not understanding how one goes about learning. He assumes, of course, that the first step is, as we have seen, the will to know the truth. Nothing can replace this. We have free wills and we can direct our minds to what we want or away from *what is* before us to something that will protect us from the whole truth.

In the beginning, Aquinas tells us that a "doctor of Catholic truth" does not direct himself to the already learned alone. He is also concerned with beginners. He teaches them things that are "congruent" to those beginning their education. Several things can impede learning. The first thing that causes difficulty, he tells us in the second paragraph of the *Summa*, is the "multiplication of useless questions, articles, and arguments." Since the *Summa*, which is to follow, itself has some ten thousand questions, articles, and arguments, we presume that the word "useless" here is not opposed to the word "useful." The fact that many questions are necessary is not a sign of fault but a sign of the real strangeness and abundance of things to be known. But still the beginning student is happy to have an orderly and manageable presentation of important issues.

The second reason for difficulty in learning is because the "order of the discipline" under question is not treated. Rather what is given to the student follows the order of the books assigned to be studied or some current event that draws popular attention. Instead of reading Aquinas or Aristotle themselves, who will form the minds in a proper order, students read "relevant" books chosen for some current issue but devoid of the broader context in which the consideration could be meaningful. I tell my students, "don't major in current events." Likewise, do not waste your time in college studying ethical or daily moral current events and think you are studying the ethics or Aquinas.

Finally, from this frequent repetition there will arise in the souls of the listeners a certain boredom and confusion. This, of course, is the reason why we should only read good or great books such as the *Summa* itself. Most universities today are so structured that they have no time for reading Aristotle or Aquinas. Rather they are boring their young students with confusing books and questions out of context, and lies about what is really important and what the mind is for. In short, to cite Lucy, "it is always better to know the truth."

It will be noticed that in reading the *Summa*, at every step of the way, Aquinas tells the beginning student just where he has been, where he is going, and what exactly he is treating of in the text before him. This text is always brief, systematic, intelligible, logical. At the beginning of the second question of the *Summa*, Aquinas gives the beginner a brief survey of what all three large books of the *Summa* contain; remember that these books contain 4006 pages.

> The principal intention of this sacred doctrine is to treat the knowledge of God, and this not only according as He is in Himself, but also according to what is proportionate to the creature . . . . To expose this doctrine, we intend in the first book to treat of God, in the second book of the movement of the rational creature to God, and finally, in the third part, to treat of Christ who, insofar as He is man, is the way for us to tend to God.[8]

8   I, 2, Proem.

Thus from the very beginning we know what we are about and how we will proceed. We are never intellectually "lost" in the *Summa*.

Consequently, it is no small thing to think and to think well and properly, to think the truth. Truth is in the judgment, as Aquinas says, in the judgment of what is and what is not, whether it is or is not. All else depends upon our ability to know the truth and to act on it, to speak of it to others as if we are talking about a reality that we, with them, objectively encounter outside of ourselves. The strangeness of things includes the effort to come to terms with this very strangeness. We do this by thinking, as Aquinas said.

"Nature did not give man claws and hides like the other animals because she gave him reason by which he can acquire these things for himself."

"According to St. Thomas, the mind acts freely of itself, but its freedom exactly consists in finding a way out to liberty and the light of day."

"It is always better to know the truth."

"The greatest good one can do to his neighbor is to lead him to the truth."

Chapter 11
WHAT MUST I *READ* TO BE SAVED?[*]

It is this same disciple who attests what has here been written. It is in fact he who wrote it, and we know that his testimony is true. There is much else that Jesus did. If it were all to be recorded in detail, I suppose the whole world could not hold the books that would be written.
— John, 21:24–25.

For this reason anyone who is seriously studying high matters will be the last to write about them and thus expose his thought to the envy and criticism of men. What I have said comes, in short, to this: whenever we see a book, whether the laws of a legislator or a composition on any other subject, we can be sure that if the author is really serious, this book does not contain his best thoughts; they are stored away with the fairest of his possessions. And if he has committed these serious thoughts to writing, it is because men, not the gods, "have taken his wits away."
— Plato, *The Seventh Letter*, 344c.

Books of travels will be good in proportion to what a man has previously in his mind; his knowing what to observe; his power of contrasting one mode of life with another. As the Spanish proverb says, "He, who would bring home the wealth of the Indies, must carry this

[*]   Lecture originally given at Rockhurst University, Kansas City, Missouri. Published on-line, Ignatius Insight, May 4, 2007.

wealth of the Indies with him." So it is in travelling; a man must carry knowledge with him, if he would bring home knowledge.
— Samuel Johnson, Good Friday, April 17, 1778.[1]

I.

We are familiar with the incident in the Gospel of the rich young man who asked Christ what *good* he must do to be saved. Christ responded to him that he must keep the commandments. This the young man had done from his youth, a fact that Christ recognized in him. Christ added, in words that still force us to distinguish between "obligation" or "duty" and something more and different from it. If he wanted to be perfect, what he should do was to sell what he had, give it to the poor, and come follow Him.

The Gospel records that the young man did not follow this proposal, rather he "went away sad," for, as it says in striking explanation, the young man "had many riches" (Matthew 19:16–23). We might suggest that this rich young man was one of Christ's conspicuous failures along with, say, Judas, one of the thieves, the scribes, Pontius Pilate, Herod, and some of His home-town relatives.

Notice that Christ did not tell the young man to become an entrepreneur so that he could create wealth to help the poor, though there is nothing wrong with this avenue. Nor did Christ "impose" a more perfect way on him. It was up to what the young man himself "wanted" to do with his life. Yet, even on reading this famous passage, a passage to which John Paul II and Pope Francis often refer when talking to youth, we have the distinct impression that the rich young man, and perhaps the world itself, missed out on something at his refusal.

If "ideas have consequences," so, possibly more so, do choices, even refusals. We can suspect that the young man's talents, without his riches, were needed elsewhere, perhaps later with Paul or Silas.

1 *Boswell's Life of Johnson* (London: Oxford, 1931), vol. II, p. 227.

Indeed, Paul was subjected to pretty much the same process, but he decided the other way, for which we can still be thankful as we read his Epistles to the Romans, Corinthians, Ephesians, Colossians, Thessalonians, to Titus, and to Timothy.

This memorable account of the rich young man reminds us that not only is the world less when we do evil, but even when we do less than we are merely invited to do. It makes us wonder whether the world is founded in justice at all, in only what we are to "render," in what we "ought" to do. Such a world would be rather dull, I think. The highest things, while not denying their acknowledged worth, may be grounded in something quite beyond justice. An utterly 'just world' may in fact be a world in which no one would really want to live. The fact that God is not defeated by evil or even by a lesser good helps us to realize, with some comfort, I confess, that we do not find only justice at the heart of *what is*. The great book that teaches this principle, above all, is C. S. Lewis' *Till We Have Faces*, a book not to be missed.

The title of my remarks today obviously plays on these words, "What must I *do* to be saved?" I ask rather, to be provocative, "What must I *read* to be saved?" I do not intend to suggest that Christ had his priorities wrong. When I mentioned this title to a witty friend of mine, she immediately wanted to know whether any of my own books were included in this category of books "necessary-to-get-to-heaven"? I laughed and assured her that indeed the *Opera Omnia* of Schall were essential to salvation!

The irony is not to be missed. We cannot point to any single book, including the bible, and say that absolutely everyone must actually read it, line by line, before he can be saved. If this were to be the case, few would be called and even fewer chosen. Heaven would alas be very sparsely populated. But I do think that between acting and reading, even in the highest things, there is, in the ordinary course of things, some profound relationship. Acting is not apart from knowing, and knowing usually depends on reading.

Concerning books and getting to heaven, however, let me note in the beginning that, statistically, most of the people in the history of mankind who have ever been in fact saved were what we today call "illiterate," good people who did not even know how to read, let alone write and write books. Christianity does not at all disdain intelligence, quite the opposite, it thrives on it. Still it does not simply identify what it means by "salvation" or "the gaining of eternal life" with education or literacy, in whatever language or discipline. In the long dispute over Socrates' aphorism that virtue is knowledge, Christians have generally sided with Aristotle, that fault and sin are not simply ignorance. Multiple doctorates, honorary or earned, will not necessarily get us to heaven, nor, with any luck, will they prevent us from attaining this same happy goal.

No doubt, throughout its history, the Christian missions in all parts of the world, not necessarily excluding the state of Missouri or the District of Columbia, have historically been concerned with precisely literacy as a way to make the Lord known and to make human beings more fully what they already are by nature. For human beings, the fullness of being ought to include the fullness of knowledge. None the less, the drama of salvation does not bypass anyone simply because he is uneducated, or only has a B.A. from some out-of-the-way college in Iowa, where I was born.

Just as there are saints and sinners among the intelligentsia, so there are saints and sinners among those who cannot read and write. Within the Christian tradition more than a suspicion exists that the more intelligent we are, the more we consider ourselves to be "intellectuals," the more difficult it is to save our souls. The sin of pride, of willfully making ourselves the center of the universe and the definers of right and wrong, is, in all likelihood, less tempting to those who do not read or who do not have doctorates in philosophy or science than it is to those who read learnedly, if not wisely. The fallen Lucifer was of the most intelligent of the angels. His first sin was in the order of thought. No academic, I think, should forget Lucifer's existence and his sobering story. It is not unrelated to a modern academic.

II.

When we examine the infinitive, "to read," moreover, it becomes clear that a difference is found between being able to read and actually reading things of a certain seriousness, of a certain depth, not that there is anything wrong with "light" reading. Indeed, the sub-title of one of my books, *Idylls and Rambles*—though again, need I remind you, a book not necessary for salvation!—is precisely "Lighter Christian Essays." The truth of Christianity is not inimical to joy and laughter. As we see in Pope Francis, it is ultimately a defender and promoter of them, including their literary expressions. I have always considered *Peanuts* and P. G. Wodehouse to be major theologians. In truth, it is the essential mission of Christian revelation to define what joy means and how it is possible for us to obtain it, that it is indeed not an illusion. The first thing to realize is that joy is not "due" or "owed" to us.

J. R. R. Tolkien, in his famous essay, "On Fairy-Stories," even invented a special word to describe this essence of Christianity. We are not, as it sometimes may seem, necessarily involved in a tragedy or a "catastrophe" but precisely in a "Eucatastrophe." The Greek prefix "eu"—as in *Eu*charist—means happy or good, the notion that, in the end, contrary to every expectation, things do turn out all right, as God intended from the beginning.[2] This is why in part the proper worship of God is our first, not our last task, perhaps even in education. In *Josef Pieper—an Anthology*, a book not to be missed, Pieper remarks further that joy is a by-product; it is the result of doing what we ought, not an object of our primary intention; ultimately, it is a gift.[3]

"Faith," St. Paul told us, "comes from hearing," not evidently from "reading," though this same Paul himself did a fair amount of writing. We presume that he intended us to read it all. It seems odd to imagine that he wrote those letters to Corinthians, Romans, Philippians, and Ephesians with no expectation of results. When Paul remarked that faith came by "hearing," he probably did not mean to say that it could not come "by reading." We do hear of people who, as they say, "read themselves into the Church."

2   J. R. R. Tolkien, "On Fairy-Stories," *The Tolkien Reader* (New York: Ballantine Books, 1968), p. 68.
3   *Josef Pieper: an Anthology* (San Francisco: Ignatius Press, 1989), pp. 33–38.

Chesterton, I think, was one of these. In classic theology, unless we receive grace, itself not of our own fabrication, we will not have faith either by hearing or by reading or, in modern times, by watching television, itself perhaps the most difficult way of all!

There are many, no doubt, who have heard but who have not believed. Paul tells of those, including himself, who at the stoning of Stephen, put their hands over their ears so they could not hear what he was saying. Alcibiades tells of doing the same thing so that he would not hear the persuasive words of Socrates. Christ said to St. Thomas the Twin, "blessed are those who have not seen but who have believed." Every time we read this passage, we are conscious that we are among those blessed multitudes who have believed but who have not seen. And even our hearing, say in preaching, say in Sunday sermons, usually comes from someone who has previously read, and hopefully read well.

The Apostle John affirms at the end of his Gospel, a document itself full of the word, "Word,"—in the beginning was the "Word," "Word" made flesh—that he in fact wrote the words that we read and that his testimony is true. He also intimates, reminiscent of Plato, that there are many things that are not recorded in books, even in all the books in the world. Yet, as the Church teaches us, what little of these things that the Lord taught and did that have in fact been handed down to us is sufficient for us. Sometimes, it is sobering to reflect that the entire corpus of the New Testament covers a mere 243 pages in the English Revised Standard Edition. We, those of who are fortunate enough to be literate, do not have to be "speed readers" to finish the New Testament many times over during our lives, even in the course of a few days.

Whether all the books ever written in this world are contained in today's libraries, or on the on-line facilities, I doubt. But a tremendous number of them are. One of the main problems with the very title of these comments has to do with the sheer amount of books available to read, and yes, to re-read. I am fond of citing C. S. Lewis' famous quip that if you have only read a great book once, you have not read it at all. This pithy remark, of course, brings up the problem of what is a great book and why great books are really "great." And even more, it asks whether great books exist that are not called great? Ought we to spend all our time, after all, on so-called "great" books? Leo Strauss once remarked that, in the end, the famed great books contradict each other, a fact that has led many a philosopher and many a student into relativism under the very aegis of philosophic greatness. There are, as I think, "great books" that are not considered "great."

In the web site of the Library of Congress, it informs us that in 1992, the Library accessioned its 100-millionth item. It added that the Library contains books in about 450 languages. I have friends who can handle fifteen or twenty languages. Some popes seem to come close to this number. But I do not know anyone who can handle 450 different languages. That takes a rather large committee. No doubt considerable numbers of books have been added since 1992, and I do not mention the books in the British Museum or the Vatican Library, or the great French, German, Spanish, American, and Italian libraries, as well as others throughout the world. I do not know if there is some mythical person who is given the Ripley "believe-it-or-not" fame for having read the most books of any man in history. But whoever this man might be, we are aware that he could have read more books than any man in history and still not know much, not know the important things.

The complete works of many men would take much of one's life just to read. If we take St. Thomas, remembering that he had no computer and that he had at most twenty six or twenty seven years of life during which he could write anything before he died in 1274 A.D., we still find it almost impossible to believe that he actually wrote what he did. What he wrote was itself clearly dependent on what he also had read and studied. It is a constant recommendation of mine that students go over to the Library and look up on the shelves the folio *opera omnia* of St. Augustine and St. Thomas, just to consider what sort of life one would have to lead in order to write, let alone understand, such a vast amount of work. Too, the students should reflect on what very different kinds of life from each other that these two great intellectual saints lived. Moreover, we shudder to think where we should be had, like the rich young man, Augustine or Aquinas chosen some other form of life, which they no doubt could have.

The story of how the works of Aristotle or Augustine were saved for posterity is itself another of the scary accounts of how we almost lost what they wrote after they wrote it. Indeed, we did lose much of what Aristotle wrote, not to mention Cicero and other important thinkers. The very dialogue of Cicero that changed the life of the young Augustine, as he tells us in *The Confessions*, is lost. We do not have it in the Library of Congress. I was once on a division of the National Endowment for the Humanities that considered grants to libraries for the physical preservation of books and newspapers.

It is astonishing over time how fragile our output of books and papers is even with great preservation efforts. And of course all our current "on-line" facilities, in which most of today's writing and publishing first appears and indeed in which it is preserved, depend on a continuous supply of electricity, not to mention computers. These latter technologies seem to defy both time and space in enabling us to send our latest thoughts around the world or across the street in an instant. The question always remains whether we have anything to say and whether what we say is true or not.

III.

On a web site one day, I came across the name of a Hong Kong movie director by the name of John Woo. Though I had never heard of him, he evidently must be a famous director for, in several entries, he is referred to as "a god among directors." This is no mean encomium. Reading further, I found a short comment of Woo himself about his film heroes. Evidently Woo, something of a philosopher, wanted to get at the essence of why his heroes are so popular. "The killer is the man," Woo explains, "who does bad things, but he wants to be good." Needless to say, this is a variety of the Robin Hood theme, if not Lucifer himself.

But I was struck by the precise words in this passage. The killer admittedly does bad things, like, I suppose, killing people. If there were no "bad" things to be done, that is, no distinction between bad and good things, the killer evidently would not have the attraction that he does. No one doubts that "bad" things have their own obscure attraction. Unfortunately today, killing certain classes of people, like unborn babies and certain of the elderly, is not considered by everyone to be a "bad" thing, or perhaps it is just one of those "bad" things we "must" do. However, if we "must" do a "bad" thing, it is difficult to classify it as evil or ourselves as free. Necessity is not a moral category, nor an accurate description of the inner workings of a free being.

I have unfortunately never seen a Woo film. But notice the peculiar way that Woo explains the outlook of the killer of men. No doubt he does "bad" things, so Woo apparently still retains some distinction between the good and the bad. I do not know if Woo makes less successful films on non-killer-types. But the killer, even in doing bad things, still "wants" to be "good." What could this "wanting" imply? This paradoxical situation could mean either that the killer would like to reform the life that leads him to kill, so he retains the intention of the good, or that goodness depends on his "wants" or "choices," not on his deeds. This latter is closer to the sin of Adam and Eve who wanted what it was to be good or evil to depend on themselves and not on nature or God.

What must I "read" to be saved? What I will call here "the Woo principle" is actually vary old, already found in Plato. This finding is why we must read him, especially if we watch Woo movies. Socrates, as we read, maintained in the *Crito* that it was never "right to do wrong." Given a choice between death and doing wrong, we should choose death, as that is not clearly wrong if we suffer it from the hands of another. It is better to "suffer" evil than to do it. No wonder Pope Benedict praised Socrates and saw his death in relation to that of Christ.

My students I ask to read what is probably the most immoral expository book in political philosophy. This is the book that states this "Woo principle" in its modern classic form, even though Plato had already formulated it. It is also a most famous and enticing book. Students are much attracted to it and by it. Many students, indeed, I have noticed, are very charmed by it. I am charmed by it myself. We are naive if we think that the difference between good and evil is always easily recognizable, let alone easy to choose between even when we do recognize it.

This book, of course, is Machiavelli's *Prince*. One of the young companions of St. Ignatius of Loyola, Peter Ribdanera, wrote a book called, *Anti-Machiavel*. Leo Strauss, in his famous book *Thoughts on Machiavelli*, called Machiavelli simply "a teacher of evil." Now, Machiavelli can, in one sense, be looked on as a handbook. The book originally was given as a gift to the ruler of Florence, almost as if perhaps he did not himself know how to rule. It sketched how a prince would sometimes, perhaps often, do bad things in order to keep in power. So long as we think it is a good thing to stay in power no matter what, then Machiavelli's advice becomes a lesson in how to do it, especially on the "no-matter-what" part of his advice. Evidently, in such a view, what makes good men to be bad princes is the restriction on their actions imposed on them by the classical distinctions of good and evil. The prince, liberated from these restriction, presumably, would be a more "successful" ruler, if not a better man.

In the course of this book, Machiavelli tells us, with some paradox, that all armed prophets succeed and all unarmed prophets fail. At first sight, this teaching will seem quite logical until we remember that Machiavelli himself was neither a prophet nor a prince. If this is the case, that he was a minor diplomat and not a prince, it seems paradoxical that he thought his own unarmed life was worthwhile. Moreover, the prince for whom he wrote the book probably did not much need his advice or even welcome it. Machiavelli hints that his real foes are men who did not write books, namely, Socrates and Christ. Both Socrates and Christ were, moreover, unarmed prophets, as was Machiavelli himself. But Machiavelli did write a book. Neither Socrates nor Christ wrote one.

What, then, can Machiavelli mean when he says that Christ and Socrates were "un-successful." Socrates needed Plato to write about him. Christ needed the Evangelists and Paul. Evidently, what Machiavelli thought he had to undermine was not the armed prophets, but the unarmed prophets. Who was Machiavelli's audience, then? Was it Lorenzo, the prince? It hardly seems likely. By writing a charming book, Machiavelli sought to entice generations of students and students-become-rulers. These readers encounter something that, if they follow its principles, will not save them. Machiavelli wrote to turn the souls of potential philosophers away from Socrates and Christ. Unless he could manage this "conversion," the world could not be built on his "modern" political principles. To follow Machiavelli's tract, we must cease to be interested, as was Socrates, in immortality, or like Christ in first seeking the Kingdom of God.

Do I think *The Prince* to be one of the books that we must "read" to be saved? I do indeed. The knowledge of what one ought not to do is not a bad thing. It can be, but as such, it is not. It is good to know the dimensions of what is persuasively wrong. We ought to encounter disorder in thought before we encounter and especially before we duplicate it in reality. It was Aristotle, I believe, who remarked that virtue can know vice, but vice does not know virtue.

III.

What must I read to be saved? When classes were over last spring, I received an e-mail from one of my students who had arrived at his home. He wrote:

> I have found something interesting while talking to my friends here at home . . . . Many of my peers have fallen into the trap of moral relativism. They have accepted education as a means to an end. It is very disheartening. I was wondering if you had . . . any . . . suggested readings for this subject of the relativism of my generation? Many of my friends feel that religion or spirituality is a private thing, and one ought not question another's belief system. Everything is personal and therefore out of the realm of criticism. I think someone wrote something about how that affirmation of morality, religion, and

ethics as a "private" enterprise, is in itself a moral statement.

No doubt the students among this audience will recognize the sentiment expressed here.

Relativism is common, even the norm today, "Does this relativism have a history?" we wonder? In 1959, The Newman Press published an English version of Jacques Maritain's *The Sin of the Angel: An Essay on a Re-Interpretation of Some Thomistic Positions.* The book was translated by William Rossner, S.J., to whom these Rockhurst lectures are dedicated. Rossner wrote a Preface to this book, dedicated to the "members of the theology and philosophy faculties at Rockhurst College."

Rossner contrasted Maritain's more familiar style in his *Reflections on America* with that of *The Sin of the Angel. The Sin of the Angel,* Rossner thought, enables us to zero in on the essential nature of sin apart from any confusion that comes from passion or our bodily existence. "The sin of the Angel is found to be fundamentally," Rossner wrote, "a life of self above all else." Ironically, I think there are some problems connected with Maritain's thesis in this little book. It has to do with whether angels could have sinned had they not been offered a higher grace, the fact remains that one of the things we need to read to be saved is precisely about sin and evil, what and why they are. Sin and evil are bad enough in themselves, as it were, but to think wrongly about what they are is perhaps even more dangerous.

In a two-frame *Peanuts*, Sally is shown sitting upright in a formal chair staring at the TV in front of her. From the TV she hears the following announcement: "And now it's time for . . ."

In the second scene Sally, with determination, points the TV changer, which looks like a gun, at the machine and firmly announces: "No it isn't!"

The last thing we see is a printed "click."[4]

---

4 Charles M. Schulz, *Could You Be More Pacific? (Peanuts* Collector Series #8; New York: Topper Books), 1991.

Sally shoots point blank to kill the monster before her. I cite this colorful little snippet in the context of "What must I read to be saved?" because it makes the graphic point that we each must simply shut things off in order to come into some possibility of knowing what *all that is* is about.

I had mentioned to my friend, Thomas Martin, at the University of Nebraska at Kearney, that we "must get someone to the book to free him." Martin replied: "We teachers are missionaries, a light in the dark electrical jungle, filled with blasting sound bites, strobe-lights and talking heads. To pry students away from the various screens where they are spectators of life to the 'examined life' is a challenge." What struck me about Martin's remark about being surrounded by "various screens" was a mental walk through the campus where in fact we encounter screens of one sort or another almost everywhere. The only salvation from being protected from reality by such screens is to become active readers and readers of things that can take us to the highest of things, the things of man and the gods, the *things that are*.

So I am going to propose, with some rashness perhaps, a brief list of ten books that, when read, will perhaps save us or at least bring us more directly to what it is that does save us, faith and grace and good sense. The writers of the books I select will all, I think, accept the proposition that saving our souls and saving our minds are interrelated. We do not live in a chaos, though we can choose one of our own making.

As some may know, in several publications I provide a somewhat variable list of "Schall's Twenty-Five Books to Keep Sane By." I am perfectly capable of finding any number of lists of ten books that would do the same thing that I have in mind. Basically, I think that if there is something wrong with the way one lives, it is because of the way one thinks. However, I am most sensitive to Aristotle's observation that often how we live and want to live prevents us from clearly looking at what is true. Our minds see the direction that truth leads and often we do not want to go there. In short, there is no way around anyone's will, but the shortest way is go follow Sally's example, click off the screens that keep us in mere spectatorship and take up the much more active occupation of reading for understanding what it is all about.

These are the ten books: 1) Chesterton's *Orthodoxy*; 2) C. S. Lewis' *Mere Christianity*; 3) E. F. Schumacher, *A Guide for the Perplexed*; 4) Fedyor Dostoveysky, *The Brothers Karamazov*; 5) Antoine St.-Exupery, *The Little Prince*; 6) Stanley Jaki, *Chance or Reality and Other Essays*; 7) Dorothy Sayers, *The Whimsical Christian*; 8) J. M. Bochenski, *Philosophy: an Introduction*; 9) Etienne Gilson, *The Unity of Philosophical Experience*; and 10) *Josef Pieper: an Anthology*. My selection includes one Russian, two Frenchman, one Hungarian, one German, one Pole, and three English. But, one might object, "What about John Paul II's *Crossing the Threshold of Hope?*" "Or Benedict's Encyclical on Love?" Read them! What about the Bible, Plato, and Aristotle? Read them. And Augustine's *Confessions*? Never to be missed.

I do not want to "defend" my list against other lists. I can make up a dozen other lists myself. The only really long book in my list is Dostoyevsky, which takes some time to read. Gilson's book requires attention but it is manageable by most people. The Jaki essays touch on the question of the sciences. The others are short, easy to read. All should be read many times. The point about this list, however, as I see it, is that if someone reads each of the books, probably in whatever order, but still all of them, he will acquire a sense that, in spite of it all, there is an intelligibility in things that does under-gird not only our lives in this world but our destiny or salvation.

Again, there is a relation between what we think and what we do. We can think rightly and still lose our souls, to be sure. But it is more difficult. The main point is that the intelligibility of revelation is also addressed to our own intelligence. We need to be assured that what we believe makes sense on any rational criteria. Lest I err, a reading of each of these books will point us in the right direction—one that indicates at the same time how much we have yet to know, including the completion of God's plan for us itself, but also how much we can know midst what often appears as a chaos of conflicting opinion.

But to obtain the impact of these readings that I intend, one does have to click off the screens and the noises that prevent us from encountering writers, often delightful writers, who so clearly wrestle with the reality of the *things that are*, including the ultimate things. "Is that everything you have to tell us?" someone might ask. It is. "Where can I get these books?" "Are not some out of print?" The finding is part of the adventure. There are libraries. Amazon.com and used book stores exist. But we are not being very practical? Here the issue is not to be "practical." Rather it is to start us on an adventure. And it is an adventure. Just click off the screen. Try it.

Chapter 12
SENECA ON PERSONAL LIBRARIES*
Some Thoughts on Reading Widely and Reading Well

I.

Let me begin by citing three items, none, at least in the beginning, from the Roman Stoic philosopher Seneca, a man who committed suicide in despair when he fell out of favor with his former pupil, the notorious Emperor, Nero. Each remark, however, I hope will serve to advert us to how much is to be known, both what is written and what is never set down, along with how our minds should relate to this vast amount of what is before us at all times, of *what is*. The first item is taken from the Web Page of the Library of Congress, the second from James Boswell's *Life of Johnson*, and the third from C. S. Lewis.

The sheer size of the first statistic humbles us before the vastness of what there is to know. "The Library of Congress," we read, "is the nation's oldest federal cultural institution and serves as the research arm of Congress. It is also the largest library in the world, with more than 130 million items on approximately 530 miles of bookshelves. The collections include more than 29 million books and other printed materials, 2.7 million recordings, 12 million photographs, 4.8 million maps, and 58 million manuscripts."

But lest we be too overwhelmed with such numbers, consider these remarks that James Boswell records on September 22, 1777:

---

* Lecture at the "Culture and Performance Series," Georgetown University, January 26, 2006. Published in *Vital Speeches*, LXXII (February 2006), pp. 249–53.

Dr. Johnson advised me today, to have as many books about me as I could; that I might read upon any subject upon which I had a desire for instruction at the time. "What you read *then* (said he,) you will remember; but if you have not a book immediately ready, and the subject moulds in your mind, it is a chance if you again have a desire to study it." He added, "If a man never has an eager desire for instruction, he should prescribe a task for himself. But it is better when a man reads from immediate inclination."[1]

Thus, while we cannot squeeze the Library of Congress into our rooms or homes, we can and should at all times have a goodly number of books of all sorts about us. Perhaps it is not necessary to read everything to know the important things.

Yet, we must never forget that not all of life is contained in books, that reality is, in fact, much greater than even we notice. C. S. Lewis put it this way in his essay, "Historicism":

A single second of lived time contains more than can be recorded. And every second of past time has been like that for every man that ever lived. The past . . . in its reality, was a roaring cataract of billions upon billions of such moments: anyone of them too complex to grasp in its entirety, and the aggregate beyond all imagination. By far the greater part of this teeming reality escaped human consciousness almost as soon as it occurred. None of us could at this moment give anything like a full account of his own life for the last twenty-four hours.[2]

We should thus never confuse the vast reality of lived human life with what we know about it from books, however valuable what

---

1   *Boswell's Life of Johnson* (London: Oxford, 1931), vol. II, p. 148.
2   C. S. Lewis, "Historicism," *Christian Reflections* (Grand Rapids: Eerdmans, 1982), p. 107.

we know from them happens to be. We are not divine providence, but we do want to know, even if not in books, what really happened to us in the past twenty-four hours.

We are then brave, if not rash, souls if we are not simply overwhelmed by the vast amount of knowledge and information available to us in all languages, from all written and on-line sources and historical records. To illustrate this point, I have cited the statistics about the holdings in the Library of Congress. I need not mention, in addition, the various university, city, and private libraries, nor the similar libraries in London, Berlin, Rome, Paris, and a thousand other places. In addition, much of this information is "on-line," available to us in our rooms or offices. Each day the volume of correspondence and communication generated throughout the world by computer internet dwarfs, if we could only collect it, almost all the knowledge collected in written books.

We could, in fact, spend our entire lives just accurately recording what we did yesterday afternoon. Of course, if we made this effort, we would have no time left for anything else but looking at ourselves looking at ourselves, a rather boring prospect. We miss much of what we actually experience if we do not write it down. Perhaps it is well that we do not know everything about everyone and everything. That is, there is a difference between information and wisdom, between what is to be known and the order of dignity of the things we know. It seems possible to know everything but what is important.

II.

What does one read when he has read, by comparison, very, very little? He could, of course, rely on chance, which may sometimes turn out to be providential. In fact, I recall once finding a novel by Aldous Huxley, of all people. I still remember its title, *Chrome Yellow*, but not what it was about. We can find the whole text of this novel on-line today through Google. It begins with a man by the name of Dennis recalling the peculiar names of stations on a little used English rail line: "Bole, Tritton, Spavin Delawarr, Knipswich for Timpany, Bowby, and, finally, Camlet-on-the-Water." Even the very reading of such names makes one want to visit these places if they still exist.

Chance reading really happens to us and can be quite significant. If we recall the scene in Augustine's *Confessions*, for instance, he was in his early thirties, at a retreat villa near Milano. In a fit of conscience and hesitation about what to do with his life, he went into the Villa Garden desperately looking for guidance. He happened onto a book containing the epistles of St. Paul. He opened the book and the first lines that struck his eyes where those famous ones from Romans telling him, in effect, to stop drinking and carousing. Not bad advice really, at any age, whether by chance or by design.

Actually, I think chance reading should be part of our reading lives. It is good sometimes just to read anything that looks interesting. Still, the whole point of the liberal arts was initially to guide us to those readings that would free us to know the truth of things. Free us from what? First, from ourselves, secondly from our ignorance about what is out there to read. Such a project had this twofold aspect, one to enable us to be free enough from our own passions and prejudices to be able to consider something contrary to our own chosen disorders of soul, something for its own sake, second to indicate that this book is to be read before that. Some things are more worthy of reading than others; even among worthy things we must choose. Even of bad or corrupting things, we need to have some accurate idea.

Some guidance in our reading is most helpful. The theoretical justification for this guided reading I learned from Yves Simon's remarks on teaching and truth in his *A General Theory of Authority*. That guidance is what, among other things, universities were for. They were to give us an opportunity, protected a bit from the pressures of the world, to read what was great even if we had never heard of it before. A university was also to provide someone, haplessly called a professor, who would assist us to read accurately what everyone else had read. Somewhere along the line of our curiosity about what to read, we began to suspect that most folks who read worthy things had likewise also read, say, Homer. They knew about Sophocles, about Cicero and Marcus Aurelius. They knew about Isaiah and the Psalms, about the New Testament, and the Fathers of the Church, Basil and Gregory and Tertullian.

Something else quickly became clear. Those who read and commented on, say Homer, people like the great Plato, were in turn read by subsequent thinkers. Aristotle read Plato who read Homer. We then discover that Augustine, who read Paul, also read Cicero, who read Plato. Cicero who studied in Greece also sent his son to study in Athens, even though young Marcus was not much of a scholar. Aquinas read Aristotle, who read Plato, who read Homer. Plato didn't much trust Homer even though, as he tells us in the Tenth Book of *The Republic,* he loved him. Aristotle tells that he loved both Socrates and Plato, but he loved truth more. Next someone tells us of Virgil who read Homer, and of Augustine who loved to read Vigil, who read Homer. But Augustine did not, as he tells us, like to study Greek, but he did love the Latin romances, Dido in particular.

III.

Thus the question came up: Is there an "order" of reading? A "canon" of things to be read? At times it seemed that anyone who read the Bible and Shakespeare was more educated than anyone who read everything else but them. Behind this canon question of what to read when so much exists to be read looms the infinite amount of things available to read. Moreover, the fact is that we can read some novels faster than we can read one question of the *Summa* of Aquinas, which is only a couple of pages long. Again, on realizing such paradoxes, we are tempted to give up, to despair.

Even if we know that our minds are by definition made to know *all that is,* we must soberly recognize our limits. We know that we only have, at most, four score years and ten, as the Bible says, much of which must be spent doing other things than reading or learning. Just because we cannot know everything, for we are not gods, it does not follow that we cannot know the most important things, the highest things, indeed something of the worth of ordinary things.

Obviously, we do not have enough time or energy to read even a small library in Boswell's chambers, let alone all that is in the Library of Congress. We know, moreover, even if we had time to do it, that intelligent reading does not consist in taking the first book on the first shelf and work our way to the last book on the last shelf. The order of titles and subjects, though not totally unrelated, is not the order of knowing. Suppose that we took the total number of pages in the Library of Congress, divided them by the total number of people in the United States, if not the world. We then assign each existing person to read constantly eight hours a day for all of their lives. The accumulated total of pages read, I suspect, still would not amount to all that is available to be read in the Library. An unread book is not active knowledge. It is just an unread book.

But again, I do not present these reflections on what is available to know as causes of despair. I am somehow exhilarated by them. When spelled out, they suggest that we are made for infinity. I do not think that it is a bad thing that so much information exists and is more available to us than to any other generation in the history of mankind. This is about the first full generation in the history of mankind that has had the computer with all its technical aspects perfected available to it twenty four hours a day since childhood. One has the impression, however, that this availability does not mean that we are more intelligent or wiser than were say, Plato, or Aristotle, or Augustine, or Aquinas, who did not have these contraptions. Many folks wring their hands and claim that we are less and less read and educated as the number of books and computers grows exponentially. Thus, we must suspect that something else is necessary. "What is it?" we wonder.

IV.

I have entitled this chapter "Seneca and Personal Libraries." I follow the spirit of the advice that Samuel Johnson gave to Boswell.

In whatever residence we live, we should strive to have all sorts of books around us on any number of diverse subjects. Indeed, I think that one of the major off-shoots of an education, be it in college or not, is the accumulation of and attention to a personal library. I am a fan of used book stores. My advice to students of any age or place is to haunt the used book stores or places where books are sold. Also I hold, again with Johnson, that we probably won't read a book if we did not buy it ourselves. Though there are exceptions, we usually won't read books just given to us. Likewise, I think that houses should not be built, rebuilt, or rented without space for books in them. We should today no more have a house without computer connections than we have one without library facilities, granted that books take more space. We can always line some wall with book shelves, as Seneca will note.

Moreover, we should probably keep a record or log at least of what we read each year, We should also probably read A. D. Sertillanges famous book, *The Intellectual Life*, as a guide to how to discipline ourselves to read over a lifetime. Furthermore, I am the fan of a daily journal. It is surprising, following what C. S. Lewis has said, how much we do *not* notice, how much we usually forget about what happens to us each day. Lives are full of history. Lives contain history. Writing a journal makes us alert to the significance of what is said to us or of what we read, say, and write. With a little frugality and diligence, moreover, we can, even if we are hard pressed for cash, accumulate a goodly number of the basic books that formed our civilization and the human mind itself.

We happily live in an era of relatively cheap and abundant books. The used book store, even the on-line one, is something of a storehouse of our culture. We can find in used book stores or library sales or on-line sales things that we should have, even if someone else threw them away or sold them for a tenth of their cost.

However, with all my enthusiasm about collecting, reading, and keeping books, I have a caveat, that is really my main theme here. For a course, I checked Google to see what is available on-line from the Roman philosopher Seneca, I came across twenty lines from his *Tranquillity of Mind* about the reading and accumulation of books.

I am conscious of my own failure to have read much before I was twenty. I know and admire people who are far more widely read than I. But I have also realized, again following Plato, that we simply will not understand many books, if we are exposed to them much before thirty or even forty, or at least if we do not read them again when we are thirty or forty. Plato himself especially falls into this category. We will miss much if we read him when we are too young, though it still may be worth looking at him at any age. Sometimes to see, we have to be ready to see, prepared to see. The experience of not seeing what is there before us to see is a basic one. Reading Aristotle for the fourth time alerts us to the fact that seeing, intellectually seeing, is something that we also must choose to do.

V.

In the fourth chapter of the ninth book of Seneca's *Tranquillity of Mind*, he began, surprisingly, by cautioning restraint in the accumulation of books. "What is the use of having countless books and libraries," he asked, "whose titles their owners can scarcely read through in a whole lifetime?" Now, I have accumulated my share of books over the years. I have remarked that we should always have on our shelves books we have not yet read as well as those we have. Indeed, I have gone so far as to affirm that when we die, we should have on our shelves books that we intended to read but to which we never found time to pick up. I consider this fact of unread books to be a sign of the ever inquisitive nature of our minds, themselves made to know *all that is*.

So, I am not totally in agreement with Seneca, but I admit he has a point. We need not, indeed probably cannot, keep every book we ever read. He continues, "the learner is, not instructed, but burdened by the mass of them, and it is much better to surrender yourself to a few authors than to wander through many." As I have gotten older, I have come to agree with this view of Seneca. But we do not find the few books to reread without wide initial experience of reading many books. What is also true is that books that we thought, on first or second reading, were not particularly good, or not even intelligible to us, have become on re-reading books that have most moved our souls.

Seneca recalls a famous incident. "Forty thousand books were burned at Alexandria; let someone else praise this library as the most noble monument to the wealth of kings, as did Titus Livius, who says that it was the most distinguished achievement of the good taste and solicitude of kings." Considerable dispute exists about just who burned this library in Alexandria, some blame Caesar himself. Also disputed is how many books were in it— some think 400,000 due to a misreading of the way Romans calculated numbers. But these questions make no difference to Seneca's main point, namely, that we can be overwhelmed by numbers of books rather than with their importance. I frankly am an advocate of both having lots of books around me, as Johnson advised, and with reading carefully a few books, as Seneca maintained.

Seneca, moreover, did not think much of the "good taste and solicitude of kings." "There was no 'good taste' or 'solicitude' about it, but only learned luxury—nay, not even 'learned', since they had collected the books, not for the sake of learning, but to make a show, just as many who lack even a child's knowledge of letters use books, not as tools of learning, but as decorations for the dining-room."

This remark reminds me of an old and perceptive Jesuit brother, deceased now, who once came into my room, lined with books from many years. He was a very short man, stood there with his hands in his pockets shrewdly looking over my shelves of books. After a minute or so, he said: "You know what I think?"

Naturally, I answered, "No."

He replied, as an abstract principle, "I think some of these professors have so many books in their room just to prove to themselves that they are doing something!"

I suspect Seneca's books in the dining room had the same effect.

Seneca comes to his point; "Let just as many books be acquired as are enough, but none for mere show." This advice is, of course, the question: "How many books are enough?" Seneca saw no reason to have elaborate book shelves piled with books of obscure authors who bored us to death and were never read. He noted that most new and stylish houses were, in his time, built with a library situated between the cold and hot baths of the Roman love for bathing. How many houses that have swimming pools, we wonder, also have libraries?

Now I think houses should be built with a place for books, be it in the dining room or off the swimming pool or wherever there is space enough. Seneca's concern for collectors who acquire books just for show is, I suppose, a worthy one. He says explicitly that what concerns him is not books but an "excess" of them. But this advice of Seneca still incites us to ask: "What are we to read?" Where are we to begin? And, I suspect, that the more important question is not what we read at nineteen. It is whether we are still reading at forty or fifty. Have we found something worth reading again and again? Or better have we realized that some things are worth reading again and again.

In conclusion, what is worth reading? The Roman historian, Tacitus, in the fifteenth book of his *Annals*, in the year 65 A. D., recounts the death of Annaeus Seneca. Nero, the Emperor, did not, in the end, see his old teacher. As Tacitus recounts it, he, "merely sent in to Seneca one of his centurions, who was to announce to him his last doom" (15.61).[3] With evident overtones to the *Phaedo* of Plato, Tacitus continues his account:

> Seneca, quite unmoved, asked for tablets on which to inscribe his will, and, on the centurion's refusal, turned to his friends, protesting that as he was forbidden to requite them, he bequeathed to them the only, but still the noblest possession yet remaining to him, the pattern of his life, which, if they remembered it, they would win a

3   Tacitus, *Annals*, 61.

name for moral worth and steadfast friendship. At the same time he called them back from their tears to manly resolution, now with friendly talk, and now with the sterner language of rebuke. "Where," he asked again and again, "are your maxims of philosophy, or the preparation of so many years' study against evils to come? Who knew not Nero's cruelty? After a mother's and a brother's murder, nothing remains but to add the destruction of a guardian and a tutor."[4]

Does our library, I ask, contain this account of Seneca's murder? Do we know of Nero's cruelty? Or that of any other tyrant? Do we know the maxims of the philosophers?

Does our personal library contain, at our fingertips, Tacitus, Seneca, Plato, the Bible, Shakespeare, Aquinas, Augustine, Aristotle, Chesterton, or the *Life of Johnson*? How do we prepare with years of study for "the evils yet to come"? Did you know that it was better to read "from immediate inclination"? Do you know the number of books in the Library of Congress? Or that "a single second of lifetime contains more than can be recorded"?

Of such are the reasons why we should have our own books, why we should read widely and read well. "Moral worth," "steadfast friendship," the "maxims of the philosophers." "If you have not a book immediately ready, and the subject moulds in your mind, it is chance if you ever have a desire to study it again." The Library of Congress contains 29 million books. "None of us could at this moment give anything like a full account of his own life for the last twenty-four hours." The last words are Seneca's: "It is much better to surrender yourself to a few authors than to wander through many."

---

4   Ibid., 15.62.

Chapter 13

ON THE USELESSNESS OF PHILOSOPHERS[*]

Or "Why Should I Listen to Lectures When I Can Read?"

Truth compelled us to say that neither a city nor a regime nor even a man will grow in perfection until some necessity thrown by chance enmeshes *those few philosophers now called not evil but useless* into taking care of their cities whether they want to or not, and the cities into obeying them, or until true love for true philosophy falls from divine inspiration into some reigning king or regent or into one of his sons. To say either or both of these alternatives cannot occur makes no sense, I maintain. If it did, they could justly laugh us to scorn for mouthing pious wishes, don't you think?
— Plato, *Republic*, 499b.

But to remember is one thing, to know another. Remembering is merely overseeing a thing deposited in the memory. Knowing is making the thing our own, not depending on the model, nor always looking over your shoulder at the teacher. "Zeno said this, Cleanthes that"—is there any difference between you and a book? How long will you learn? Begin to teach! One man objects, "*Why should I listen to lectures when I can read?*" Another replies, "The living voice adds a great deal." It does

[*] Given as the Annual Folwell Lecture at St. Ambrose University, Davenport, Iowa, May 4, 2011.

indeed, but not a voice which merely serves for another's words and functions as a clerk.
— Seneca, "Maxims," Letters.[1]

I.

On Easter Day, April 16, 1775, Samuel Johnson attended the services in St. Paul's Cathedral in London. Later, he dined with Boswell and Mrs. Williams. After conversing on the notion of happiness in the Roman poet, Horace, they talked about reading. Some people in their circle evidently thought that, for gaining wisdom and knowledge, conversation was enough. Johnson doubted that conversation, however important, was adequate.

> "The foundations must be laid by reading," Johnson observed. "General principles must be had from books, which, however, must be brought to the test of real life. In conversation you never get a system. What is said upon a subject is to be gathered from a hundred people. The parts of a truth, which a man gets thus, are at such a distance from each other that they never attain to a full view."[2]

The indispensability of reading, even for conversation, is what I want to talk about here at St. Ambrose.

And, yes, books do need, as Johnson observed, to stand "the test of real life." The common man's instinctive skepticism of the academic is not wholly misplaced. Many silly things can be found in scholarly books, of course, along with many a subtle error convincingly, even elegantly, expressed.

Yet, I maintain that truth ultimately exists in conversation. It needs to come alive when someone is actually knowing, speaking,

---

1   Seneca, "*The Stoic Philosophy of Seneca,* translated by M. Hadas (New York: Norton, 1958), p. 187.
2   *Boswell's Life of Johnson* (London: Oxford, 1931), vol. I, p. 592.

and hearing it. That is when it is luminous precisely as truth. The definition of man, as Robert Sokolowski writes, is that he is "an agent of truth." Each person brings it forth out of its silence in his reading, knowing, and speaking.[3]

"Without truth language would be a general fog of words above the silence," Max Picard wrote; "without truth it would collapse into an indistinct murmuring. It is truth that makes language true and firm."[4] The old Beatles song spoke of the "sounds of silence." We hear many things when we are still. Cicero told us at the beginning of his treatise, "On Duties," that he was "never less alone than when he was alone." In silence he was listening to what he read, to what was addressed to him that he often could not hear because of the surrounding noise.

Reading is not exactly speaking to ourselves. Rather it is closer to "listening" to someone of almost any time or place "speaking" to us through his written words. These words echo in us out of their silence when we read them. They are charged with reality. They bear meaning. Nietzsche said that "In antiquity, when a man read—which he did very seldom—he read to himself aloud."[5] We might try that.

Reading aloud is, I think, the first step, the concern that someone else hears the words we speak. Understanding follows words, as words bear the meaning of what they symbolize, of what is there. What we have read provides the storehouse of memory on which intelligence and experience rely. Memory permits us to draw on some source beyond that of our immediate context. So we need to consider the import of books, books that we can touch and keep and, yes, read again. The keeping of books is a fine art, only subordinate to the finer art of knowing which ones to keep.

As you know, though in my Iowa youth I never made it as far east as Davenport, after beginnings in Pocahontas and Eagle Grove,

3   Robert Sokolowski, *The Phenomenology of the Human Person* (New York: Cambridge, 2008).
4   Max Picard, *The World of Silence* (Wichita: Eighth Day Press, [1948] 2002), p. 31.
5   Frederick Nietzsche, *Beyond Good and Evil* (Harmondsworth: Penguin, 1974), #247, p. 160.

I went to grammar and high school in Knoxville, Iowa, which is west of Davenport, over by Des Moines, but in this diocese. We had a public library there. I believe that it was founded during the Depression with funds provided in part by a program of the Carnegie Foundation. I tried to check this history.

When I "googled" "History of Public Library, Knoxville, Iowa," I received the following response: "'History of Knoxville Library' returns no results." Alas, the library of my Iowa youth apparently has no history! And in that on-line response, the word "library" was spelled "libraery"! I suddenly became concerned about the validity of my high school diploma!

But I do remember that library, however it is spelled. It is still a rather handsome, solid building. I recall looking up books when I had no idea about what I was looking for, not a totally unhealthy condition. If we only read books we knew about ahead of time, we would, I think, live very narrow lives. This initial not-knowing what is in a library or book store, or even worse, of not knowing what to read, is a necessary stage in every man's intellectual life. In the Knoxville Library, I remember reading many of James Oliver Curwood's dog stories like *Kazan, Son of the North*.

In high school, I even remember, during World War II, checking out a book written by none other than Joseph Stalin. I was even impressed with it; such is the innocence of a Knoxville youth. It is not altogether a bad thing to run across huge errors before you have sense enough to know that they are either errors or huge. Yet, all in all, I was not at the time a diligent reader. No doubt, a fine line exists between the desire to read and the assignments of something to read. But the mere capacity to read at all is one's real ticket to *all that is*, to the worlds of other lives and times and places.

Our literature, after all, is filled with stories of young men and women, caught in large houses or mansions in which many books look down on them from high shelves. Suddenly on finding *The Three Musketeers* or *Oliver Twist* or even the *Journals of Lewis and Clark*, they spend hours and days with them, happily lost in another time and place. The only way we can really appreciate our own time and place is to realize that other times and places meant much to others of our kind. Through books we can live in our own way lives that are not ours. We can become more than we are while retaining ourselves to be what we already are from our beginning.

Of late, I have been enchanted with Christopher Morley's 1917 novel *Parnassus on Wheels*, a reprint of which someone from out of nowhere gave me. It is a charming story about a used bookstore on wheels. It is pulled by a horse with the name of Peg through the outlying farms and towns on Long Island. When Parnassus pulls up into their yards, Professor Mifflin seeks to convince the skeptical but shrewd farmers of Long Island to look to books.

Mifflin puts it this way: "You are all used to hucksters and peddlers and fellows selling every kind of junk from brooms to bananas. But how often does anyone come around here to sell you books? You've got your town library, I dare say; but there are some books that folks ought to own."[6] Now, even in this world of online everything that can take us anywhere, I think it is still true that "there are some books that folks ought to own." It took me a while after the Knoxville Public Library before I learned the truth of this advice. Nothing is lonelier, I think, than a house with no books or provisions for them. Never plan to live in one.

II.

In the beginning of these reflections, I cited a passage from the Roman philosopher Seneca, a man who was, as we saw earlier from Tacitus, eventually disposed of by his former pupil, the notorious Emperor Nero. Professors can never be too careful about who sits out there in their classes! In this citation, the question was asked, "Why should I listen to lectures when I can read?" Here we are, aren't we, listening to a lecture about reading. Words need the "living voice," but it needs to be a voice that indicates a comprehension of what is the subject of our discourse. Babbling is not conversation.

6   Christopher Morley, *Parnassus on Wheels* (England: Dodo Press, 1917, Reprint), p. 30.

Human life indeed should have ample place for lightsome and even frivolous interchanges among us. Yet, conversation presupposes meditation and the pondering of things in our own souls, important things, but, as I said, not only important things. I am always struck by the wonder of unimportant things. They too are part of the fabric of our being. Our world is not a parsimonious one cut clear of all superfluities by Occam's famous razor that did not want to multiply things unless by necessity. Rather our world and our lives are filled with an astonishing abundance almost as if to say that no way can be found for us to grasp the full wonder of all the *things that are*.

A cartoon in the *New Yorker* shows a rather astonished and ill-sorted couple sitting in their living room with their huge dog. The wife is reading out loud to her pipe-smoking husband a letter from their daughter away in college—no doubt not St. Ambrose! The daughter is reporting on her grades and on the course titles that she is taking: "Sarah's grades are excellent," the mother says. "She got A+ in 'Yogi Berra: Philosopher or Fall Guy?', A in 'Dollars and Scents: An Analysis of Post-Vietnam Perfume Advertising', A- in 'The Final Four as Last Judgment: The N.C.A.A. Tournament from a Religious Perspective', and A in 'The American Garage Sale: Its Origin, Cultural Implications, and Future'."[7]

As I look at these wonderful, outlandishly titled courses, whose listings are not totally unobserved on class pre-registration days, I recall the advice that I give my students, to wit: "Whatever you do in college, do not major in current events." Suppose a student's semester program of five classes looks like this: 1) "History of Islam in Algeria"; 2) "Earth Warming Science"; 3) "Power Relations in Eudora Welty"; 4) "A Survey of Obama's Best Speeches"; and 5) "Drug Wars in Mexico." Such a program is practically useless. It will be obsolete the day the student graduates, if not sooner. It will be replaced by other equally ephemeral topics.

The whole purpose of college is to protect students from current events for long enough that they can acquire some perspective

---

7 Booth, *The New Yorker Book of Teacher Cartoons* (New York: Bloomberg Press, 2006), p. 39.

on the human condition as an abiding thing through time. The term "liberal" in liberal education means to be free from ephemeral things long enough to catch a glimpse of the highest things.

When we take St. Augustine in class, I say to my students: Supposing St. Augustine were to return to life today and, over a cup of coffee, were to read the *Washington Post, The New York Times*, and *Le Monde*. Would anything in those papers really surprise him? The answer is really: "No." There, he would read of wars, political corruption, frivolities, moral abuses, envy, as well as few nice things, the same things he would have read in his day in Carthage, Rome, Milano, or Hippo Regius.

In a way, we should be reading at least some things that no one will tell us about. I envision the sad case of the student who graduates from an expensive college. But, on receiving his diploma, he has yet read nothing of Plato, Aquinas, Chesterton, Dickens, Dante, Shakespeare, Samuel Johnson, or Isaiah. Moreover, there is simply no such thing as a university in the proper sense in which the constant reading of Plato is not going on. But it is not always easy. It took me years and years before I ever began to appreciate Plato. Now, in my declining years, I sometimes wonder whether I should bother teaching anything else but Plato.

III.

In the second volume of Benedict XVI's *Jesus of Nazareth*, he tells us that it is possible, as it were, to hear across the ages. "I have attempted to develop a way of observing and listening to the Jesus of the Gospels," Benedict explains, "that can indeed lead to personal encounter and that, through collective listening with Jesus' disciples across the ages, can indeed attain sure knowledge of the real historical figure of Jesus."[8] This approach is not "*sola scriptura.*" But it does call our attention to the book, to the reading, to the aliveness of what is there for us to discover through words.

8   Benedict XVI, *Jesus of Nazareth* (San Francisco: Ignatius Press, 2011), vol. II, p. xvii.

In the first passage that I cited in the beginning from Plato, we found the famous passage in which Socrates said that most people suspected that most philosophers were useless. Socrates told us, moreover, that none of us wanted to be laughed to scorn for mouthing pious wishes. Among these pious wishes was found the possibility that divine inspiration might fall to one of the sons of a king. Christians read that passage with considerable astonishment.

With such inspiration, the inspired king might be able to see the truth and hence pass it along to others over whom he ruled. Rulers must be found who "take care of their cities." The politician is mostly too busy really to know in what this care consists. He is too overwhelmed with pressing things which are sometimes also ultimate things. The salvation of the city is not in the city's hands alone. Indeed, the city cannot properly speaking be saved. Only individual persons can. The philosopher, however, if he be true to the evidence, had glimmerings of a truth that transcended the city.

Early in the fall semester of grammar school, Charlie Brown and Lucy are coming home from class. Walking behind Lucy, Charlie complains, "Homework already! Write a thousand word essay on what we did during the summer!"

Lucy turns around as Charlie continues, "NOBODY can write a thousand word essay on what he did during the summer! It's ridiculous!"

But everyone knows that the ridiculous happens all the time in grammar schools throughout the world. They continue walking. Charlie next asks Lucy, "When are you going to try to write yours, this evening?"

With some prissiness of which she is famous, Lucy replies, "Mine's already finished. I wrote it during study period!"

In frustration, Charlie then screams at her, "YOU DRIVE ME CRAZY!!!"

Charlie next turns to Linus for sympathy. "Do you know why English teachers go to college for four years?"

Puzzled, Linus replies, "No, I don't know why English teachers go to college for four years."

Charlie explains, "Well, then I'll tell you why English teachers go to college for four years."

At this he yells out to a bowled-over Linus, "SO THEY CAN MAKE STUPID LITTLE KIDS WRITE STUPID ESSAYS ON WHAT THE DID ALL STUPID SUMMER!!"[9]

So much for relevance essays!

Yet, as I think of this wonderful scene, the principal elements of what I want to stress are already here. The purpose of college education is not to make stupid kids write stupid essays about what they did all stupid summer. But the purpose might just be to write an intelligent essay about anything, including what we did last summer. Anything human and, yes, anything divine, are, after all, the proper subject matter of our curiosity and of our writing.

No college education is complete which, like Charlie Brown with Lucy, lacks that sense of being driven crazy by students who are brighter than they are. The worst thing that can happen to us is never to meet anyone more intelligent than we are. Usually we meet many such in our allotted time but we do not recognize them. It is not good for our vanity to admit our limitations, but it is good for our souls.

A sure test that we are not really interested in truth is when we envy those who really do know more than we do. This is why in the classical rankings of the vices, envy is much worse than greed or lust. It is a purely spiritual vice that refuses honor where honor is due to the truth of a thing.

IV.

We should indeed listen to lectures even when we can read them. We need to hear spoken to us what we do not yet know. Philosophers are "useless." That is the best thing about them. They do not properly belong to Aristotle's categories of the useful or the pleasurable. They are interested in truth "for its own sake," as Aristotle also told us.

---

9   Charles Schulz, *Peanuts Treasury* (New York: Fall River Press, 2005).

In a recent essay in the *New York Times* (March 5, 2011) by Bob Herbert entitled, "College the Easy Way," we learn that "for a large portion of the nation's seemingly successful undergraduates the years in college barely improve their skills in critical thinking, complex reasoning and writing." The situation evidently looks bleak. "Students are hitting the books less and partying more. Easier courses and easier majors have become more and more popular. Perhaps more now than ever, the point of the college experience is to have a good time and walk away with a valuable credential after putting in the least effort possible."

I would be more sympathetic of this kind of criticism did I not suspect that the phrase "critical thinking, complex reasoning and writing" contained an agenda that is not obvious or neutral. The chief engine that powers a humanist agenda that has no connection with human nature or the transcendent order comes from universities that push this "critical thinking" into areas where it does not belong. We are not simply talking about Socrates with his dialogues here. We need places where we can, as it were, critique "critical thinking" and the "complex reasoning and writing" that accompany it.

We might well argue that the reason that students take such "fresh air courses," as they are called, is not because they are only interested in partying or having a pleasant four years at their parents' or government's expense. They do so because there is nothing being taught in these places of leaning that gets to the heart of things worth knowing for human living. If what is taught in our universities is basically relativism, sophism, or positivism, as it mostly is, it is perfectly normal to be bored to death with it. This was Allan Bloom's point in his *Closing of the American Mind*. Rather, we are in dire need, as Plato said, of "true love for true philosophy." The reason we do not find the highest things discussed is because we cannot consider all the sources of knowledge including revelation directed to reason.

As a result, we usually have to study the highest things on our own. This is why we need to know about books and teachers that are not often found in the universities. Universities usually produce professors who replicate themselves, their intellectual presuppositions, over time. Our souls burn to know the truth. But the burning dies out if we are constantly told that there is no truth or that everything is power and self-interest.

Students are told directly or indirectly that there is no truth. They listen to what is taught. Any fool can draw the logical consequences of that proposition for his own life. Nothing really matters. Why not have a good time? Max Picard put it well: "'There is no truth,' said one. The other said: 'But you are yourself assuming that it is a truth that there is no truth.'"[10] This is nothing else but the classical refutation of skepticism. Once a student understands the truth of this proposition, he is free to look elsewhere, to places where truth can be found and delighted it.

In conclusion, we read in the Book of Ecclesiastes (c. 6): "Better the end of a speech than its beginning." We are indeed at the end of this lecture. "So, why should I listen to lectures when I can read?" Or "Why do English teachers go four years to college?" Why not study the "Final Four as Last Judgment" if we cannot study the Last Judgment as theology, as Benedict XVI did in *Spe Salvi*? And why on earth should anyone listen to a lecture, like this one, when some professor, even if he was born in Iowa, tells us that philosophy is precisely "useless"?

The answer, I think, is that we really do want to know the truth of things. "'There is no truth,' said one. The other said, 'But you are yourself assuming that it is true that there is no truth.'"

This is why we are "driven crazy," as Charlie Brown said. The very nature of our being is unsettled until we stand in truth. Saint Augustine said the same thing long ago. He said it better than anyone since. He said that "Our hearts are restless until they rest in Thee," one of the most quoted sentences in all our literature.

No university or other kind of education that does not know this metaphysical restlessness about ourselves will ever be anything but boring. In the end, I think, I am on the side of the students who find little substantial in their courses from those professors who

10   Picard, p. 32.

spend their days with "critical thinking" that, in the end, is said to prove that nothing true can be known anyhow, only what is useful. As Plato said, "truth compels us." We seek "true love for true philosophy." In the end, we suspect that "divine inspiration" has something to do with it, as it does with our restless hearts.

Chapter 14
BUT WHAT *IS* A BOOK?[*]

Dr. Johnson advised me to-day, to have as many books
about me as I could; that I might read upon any subject
upon which I had a desire for instruction at the time.
"What you read then (said he,) you will remember; but if
you have not a book immediately ready, and the subject
moulds in your mind, it is a chance if you again have a
desire to study it." He added, "If a man never has an
eager desire for instruction, he should prescribe a task for
himself. But it is better when a man reads form immediate
inclination."
— James Boswell, Monday, September 22, 1777.[1]

Someone who denies there is anything essential in things
would have to assert that there is really no difference between a scatterbrained, loose, associative account of a
topic, and an account in which the thing is effectively presented. He would have to say there is no difference between a speech in which the speaker never gets to the
point and one in which the point is clearly made. No one
can really deny that such differences exist."
— Robert Sokolowski, *Pictures, Quotations, and Distinctions*, 1992.[2]

---

[*]   Lecture given at Dartmouth College, May 3, 2012.
[1]   *Boswell's Life of Johnson* (London: Oxford, 1931), vol. II, p. 148.
[2]   Robert Sokolowski, *Pictures, Quotations, and Distinctions*: Fourteen Essays
       in Phenomenology (Notre Dame: University of Notre Dame Press, 1993), p.
       105.

> At that time . . . the only thing that pleased me in Cicero's book [the lost *Hortensius*] was his advice not simply to admire one or another of the schools of philosophy, but to love wisdom itself, whatever it might be, and to search for it, pursue it, hold it, and embrace it firmly.
> — St. Augustine, *Confessions*, III, 4.[3]

I.

No one, I think, with any sense of history and propriety, can come to Dartmouth College for the first time and not recall Daniel Webster's remark that it is "but a small college but there are those of us who have loved it." I am sure Dartmouth students have heard this passage many times. The remark still moves my soul whenever I come across it. Dartmouth still boasts that it is the smallest of the Ivy League schools, though, with some four to six thousand students, it is only "small" when compared to, say, Ohio State or NYU or Texas.

Dartmouth's smallness is mindful to me of Chesterton's remark that Rome was not first great and then men loved her. Rather they first loved her, then, as a result, she became great. To stay sane, we always need to get our metaphysical priorities right. That was Webster's point too, I think. Much is to be said for a man who loves a woman because she is beautiful. But, as Yves Simon said, much more is to be said of him when he still faithfully loves her when she has lost her beauty.

We do not love, at least properly, the qualities of something but the thing itself, *what is*. Things are not loveable because we make them loveable. They are first loveable because of what they are, because each thing, in its own kind, already is the result of a love that constitutes *what it is*. We cannot love unless we are first loved. We only discover what is already there. *Omne ens est bonum*—everything that exists is good. Though it is up to us what we do with the love in which we are initially created, we cannot deny our

3   St. Augustine, *The Confessions* (London: Penguin, 1961), p. 59.

origins. We can, indeed and, alas do, make ourselves less worthy of what we ought to be. We call this capacity, or at least its source, freedom. It is the first thing that God respects because, without it, the purpose for which we exist cannot in fact be achieved.

I have entitled this chapter: "What *Is* a Book?" Thus, I am asking what Leo Strauss called a *"what is?"* question. Why does something, including a book, exist at all? Why is this thing this not that thing? "What is" questions ask the "form" or formal cause question: *What is it?* "What is?" questions imply "is it?" answers. Is it? Or Is it not? *"Why is it?"* questions take us to the heart of their very existence, to the meaning of existence itself. So a book is an artifact, a product of human ingenuity. What it is makes it a book, not a turtle or a hay barn.

A book does not exist without an agent who wants to say something to others, to express something in what he takes to be an organized, coherent form. He must arrange that what he wants to say appears in the world in a form that others can see and read. Here is where book publishers come in or other forms of communication. Once a book exists in a language that at least some few can understand, it is designed to be read by other human beings, though I imagine there are existing, published, not to mention unpublished, books that have never been read or only read a few times. Though we still read it, Nietzsche's *Beyond Good and Evil* was author-published in German with 118 copies printed. Not a few books are unread in the lifetime of their authors. Others are never read one or two years, sometimes months, after their publication. Depositories of read and unread books are called libraries.

And yes, some books move our souls and we cannot forget them. Charlie Brown is reading a book to Schroeder who is attentively listening. He reads: "At the conclusion of the symphony the audience stood up and cheered." In the second scene, Charlie goes on while Schroeder is riveted to the account. "Beethoven, however, because of his deafness, could not hear them, and because his back was to the audience, could not see them." The third scene continues: "With tears on her eyes, one of the singers led Beethoven to the edge of the stage where he could see the cheering people . . ."

The final scene is touching. Schroeder simply buries his face in his hands sobbing while Charlie looks on with some puzzlement.[4] Books, even reading from them, can do this to us; they can put us there where we are not. Like Schroeder we too are tempted to weep on hearing such a passage.

II.

The philosophical act, as Robert Sokolowski says, is "to distinguish." *This* is not *that*. The human mind as mind becomes fully what it is when it, as it were, is full of understood distinctions, fully aware of the differences and similarities of things. All things that exist simply *are*. Their "are-ness" manifests itself in what they do. What they can do flows from what they already are. *Agere sequitur esse*, as the classical statement of the principle went. The action of a thing flows from *what it is*.

Now, a book is, at first sight, an artifact, something ultimately made by the being with mind and hand, as Aristotle define our unique nature. A book does not grow on trees, though, in a sense, we can call it a "living" thing. As intelligible, it only exists when it is being known by a writer or reader. As E. F. Schumacher said, more or less, if you give a monkey a copy of *Hamlet*, he may throw it, eat it, or sit on it, but he won't read it. The plot of *King Lear* is the same in English and in German, in Kindle form or in an elegant edition from the Folio Society of London.

I do not personally possess such a Folio volume of *Hamlet*. But I do have the Folio Society's edition of P. G. Wodehouse's wonderful *Leave It to Psmith*, a book I wonder whether it can be translated into German at all. But since most Germans read English, there is little need. This Wodehouse is one of the Blandings Castle series with Lord Eamsworth, who is described as a "fluffy-minded man with excellent health and a large income." In any case, the hero of this famous book to whom we are to "leave it" spells his name "P-s-m-i-t-h." Much to our orthographic relief, however, we are soon

4 Charles M. Schulz, *The Complete Peanuts*, 1955–56.

informed that the P is "silent" in Psmith. Was there ever a more curious or provocative name in the title of any book, I wonder? But of course, this title is a parody on a 1933 English play entitled, naturally, *Leave It to Smith*, with no "P." I believe the original "Smith," unlike the Wodehouse "Psmith," was a rather responsible gentleman to whom one could safely "leave things" and, lo, they would be done.

The Library of Congress, as we mentioned earlier, contains something over thirty-five million books. About five hundred and thirty-eight miles of book shelves are found in this Library. Yet, today, all of these books could probably be digitalized and housed in something the size of the London Folio Society's edition of *Leave It to Psmith*.

Moreover, books are no longer physical items, things written on stone, sheepskin, or paper. They are first blips on a computer screen that, once written, are later put to paper, if necessary. The paperless society gets along without books. Nothing prevents a book to be written and read solely in its lightsome on-line form. I do columns and essays all the time that only have on-line existence. Paper books of various sizes, shapes, and durability are still, thank goodness, with us. They may still be preferred in this solid form by many as the way to read and keep knowledge. I do not look forward to the day, already here in principle, when the only way that I can make inexpensively available the ten to twelve books that I usually assign to a semester class is to put them on Kindle where they exist, not as my physical, tangible book, but as a right to read an image.

III.

I began this lecture with a citation from Boswell that I often quote. He recalls that Samuel Johnson advised him always to have plenty of books at hand so that wherever one's curiosity leads him, he can easily find what he is looking for. Often I stand outside of a class talking to several students, at least some of whom will have their cell phones in hand. If the conversation dulls or the phone gongs, out will come the phone. On most campuses and streets today, it is very difficult to say hello to anyone as everyone seems to be walking down the street looking at his cell phones. These instruments isolate people as much as they expand their scope.

But if, for instance, someone wants to know who the losing pitcher in the last game of the World Series in 1937 was, within twenty seconds, one of the students will consult his cell phone to come up with the answer. I had to look it up on Google. The loser was Cliff Melton of the New York Giants. The Yankees' winning pitcher was Lefty Gomez, a name I remember from my youth.

Every statistic about that 1937 World Series game is in the *Baseball Almanac*, which is now on-line. Indeed, I presume today that on-line somewhere you can now actually find a video version of every game of any World Series in recent years. What does this availability of all facts in non-book, immediately-accessible form mean? It means that, if you know how to ask the right question on an electronic device, very few factual things are not findable in a few seconds.

The on-line world takes the place of books, or it is another form of a book, depending on how one looks at it. In a sense, it also, to recall Book Ten of Augustine's *Confessions*, takes the place of memory itself. Why remember what you can look up, usually with a more accurate answer? The man who once was famous for keeping baseball statistics in his head is now obsolete, as is his head unless we come up for some other purpose for knowing and remembering just facts. That things are in our memories and not just on a machine means that they are immediately related to all else we know.

So, I do not think that Johnson's advice to Boswell was a mere question of availability of facts. Johnson talks of the man who "does not have an eager desire for instruction." It may help him if he has a book list and disciplines himself to read the ones listed. Still, Johnson thought, "It is better when a man reads form immediate inclination." I presume that the visible medium that a man uses, book or electronic device, does not matter. The matter read is the same. Education cannot mean teaching us just to use a computer so that we can look up facts quickly and deftly. The essential thing is the "inclination," or even better "the immediate inclination." And this "inclination" can be nothing other than the desire to know and retain the truth of things, of *what it is*.

From whence, we might ask, does this "immediate inclination" come? Aristotle simply said that man is by nature a rational animal. Johnson here is not against the experience we all have had of reading a book that someone gave us that we had no intention of reading, or had never heard of, but we decided to read it anyhow. And, lo, on reading it, we were quite taken with it. That experience used to happen in libraries when we went in to find one book and, by chance, pulled down another sitting near it that we had long wondered about. We called it browsing, something, interestingly enough, we still use in computers.

The human mind as such, as Aristotle tells us, is *capax omnium*, a capacity or power to know all things. This means primarily knowing the relation of things one to another. All things are knowable. Each is this thing, not that. We distinguish. The very act of knowing is one of wonder and contemplation that something *is*. We just want to know. Yet, we have to "intend." We have to be gripped by the unsettlement of not knowing and the corresponding pleasure of knowing. Like all pleasures, the pleasure of knowing follows on and is intrinsic to the act of knowing, which is not as such simply pleasure. Some things we want to know, Aristotle told us, even if they are painful.

IV.

I have spent a good deal of my life recommending books to read. In several of my books I include lists of books to read. I do not consider myself to be a voracious reader, though I have, somehow, had in my days a considerable time in which to read. The religious and academic lives lend themselves to having this reading time, as can a long life. What has interested me more is *what* to read. I have read Anne Fadiman's delightful book, *Ex Libris: Confessions of a Common Reader*. This too is a book about books.

I recall that when I was in college at Santa Clara that a wise professor gave us to read Mortimer Adler's *How to Read a Book*, ironically a rather difficult book to read if there ever was one. A friend of mine, Peter Redpath, has even written a useful little volume called *How to Read a Difficult Book*. Yet, not all the most important books to read are "difficult." What are called "great books" are not the only ones worth reading and indeed as Leo Strauss pointed out, the great books often contradict each other and tempt us unnecessarily to skepticism.

So again, what is a book? At the beginning of the *Summa Theologiae*, a book intended for beginners, a book of no fewer than 4,006 folio pages, Thomas Aquinas gave a few observations on why students might have a trouble reading. One reason was that we need to understand the natural order of a discipline. What is it about? He also thought that many books are filled with things that are really not pertinent to the topic at hand. He himself seems to have memorized most of Scripture, Aristotle, and about everything else he read, while, at the same time, composing a vast library of books in less than the twenty-five years allotted to him in divine providence.

A book can be a tightly organized argument with a thesis that carefully goes through its evidence in a logical and coherent manner. The second citation that I began with was a passage from a very interesting book by Robert Sokolowski, *Pictures, Quotations, and Distinctions*. A picture communicates to us also, but in a different way than a book or writing does. A portrait of a given person tells us something about than person that no amount of writing can. But writing can tell us of his thoughts and insides in a way that pictures cannot. Indeed, most pictures need some words so that we know what we are looking at.

Drawing on common experience, Sokolowski asks us to consider the case of someone who denies that we can know anything essential from things. No order or reason is found in things. In explaining this theory to us, the man would imply that any written account of things would make no difference whether it was scatterbrained or coherent. We would have nothing against which to check the two accounts. Or take the difference between a speech that is rambling and one that is organized. The mere fact that we can recognize the difference between these diverse situations means that we have implicitly a standard against which to measure words, written or spoken. Since we can tell the difference between these two, it follows that there is order or coherence in what they describe, otherwise we would not be able to distinguish one thing from another. Nothing we say would have any meaning. There would be no sense in speaking to anyone of anything.

V.

The last citation in the beginning is a famous passage from Augustine's *Confessions*. It is Augustine's recollection of an incident in his early life when he was about eighteen or nineteen. Augustine lived in a back country town called Tagaste and went to school in nearby Madurae, both in present day Algeria. The big city was nearby Carthage, in modern Tunisia, a famous place to which he was soon to flee and then on to Rome and Milano.

Augustine seems to have been teaching rhetoric, basically how to be a lawyer, how to speak and argue in public, not just for money, but for glory and fame. While he was there, he chanced to come across a dialogue of Cicero, called the *Hortensius*. Though Hortensius was a famous lawyer who was to oppose Cicero in the famous case *Against Verres*, concerning the corruption of the Senate, this dialogue, now lost, was about philosophy.

I bring this scene up here because of Samuel Johnson's notion that we should read "from immediate inclination," that is, because we are moved by what we read. When Augustine put down his copy of the *Hortensius*, some four hundred years after it was written, he, Augustine, decided that he wanted to be a philosopher. So a precocious young man, in a remote corner of the Empire, by chance finds a book, which he reads. Augustine certainly knew and was charmed by Cicero, but this was a new revelation to him. The world would be changed because Augustine read a book and wanted thence to be a philosopher.

Changes in the world first take place in the souls of men. What causes us to be good or evil will happen to us in a given time and a given place. The factors that brought the changes about will look from the outside to be accidental. And they are in one sense. The world was changed when the young Augustine decided to be a philosopher. To be sure, in the beginning he was a very bad philosopher. But he was also brilliant and eventually able to think out of bad philosophy to explicate things on the reading of which we are still mostly in awe.

But, again, what is a book? A book is something that can change the world because it records the ideas of men, ideas that can be tested for coherence or incoherence, truth or falsity because of the order of things. When I was in the hospital not too long ago, a friend gave me a mystery story to read. Christopher Morley's *The Haunted Bookstore* was written in 1918, about a bookshop in Brooklyn. The owner of the shop was a devoted reader of books and collected them to resell. Into his shop one evening came a young man who, in chatting with the owner, supposes that a book store is a dull place. "Far from it," Mr. Mifflin, the owner, replies, "Living in a bookshop is like living in a warehouse of explosives. Those shelves are ranked with the most furious combustibles in the world—the brains of men."[5] A book is explosively loaded with the brains of men.

Let me conclude with another story from Augustine, this time from Book Eleven (chapter 28) on time in the *Confessions*. Suppose we have something memorized, he tells us. Let it be a familiar psalm, itself taken from the Book, the Good Book, the Bible. The word, bible, comes from the name of the Phoenician port of Byblos from which parchment was sent to Greece for writing purposes. And "Bible" as a book is itself only written after men had remembered, organized what they had seen, heard, and passed it down.

The psalm exists word for word in our memory. We can recite it. Before we recite it, it is in the future. After we recite it, it is in

---

5   Christopher Morley, *The Haunted Bookshop* (New York: J. B. Lippencott, 1919), p. 25.

the past. While we recite it is in the now as passing. But we remember the before and after. The same time sequence happens even in a word or syllable. While he is reciting the psalm, Augustine tells us, "my faculty of attention is present." The psalm passes into our memory, where it remains as a whole that we have to recall and recite one word at a time. We find something we encounter, memorize, know. We recite it step by step from future to past.

What is the significance of this experience or reading aloud or silently a whole psalm or a poem? It is not unlike the remark of Sokolowski about seeing the intelligence in what we read and what this intelligence presupposes about reality. "What is true of the whole psalm is also true of all its parts and in each syllable," Augustine tells us. "It is true of any longer action in which I may be engaged and of which the recitation of the psalm may only be a small part. It is true of a man's whole life, of which all his actions are parts. *It is true of the whole history of mankind, of which each man's life is a part.*"

That is a remarkable passage. The thought that I want to leave you with is this: I noticed that passage in a book that I had read many times before. But I had never really "seen" and pondered it before. It is a passage that directly connects my life, any life, with the whole history of mankind.

At eighteen, Augustine decided to be a philosopher. He got the idea from a book written four hundred years before his time. I learned this fact from reading a book that Augustine wrote when he was in his early fifties while reflecting on his early life. I read this book with a class some fifteen hundred years after Augustine wrote it. What is contained in books are the considered "brains of men." Books, if not brains, are indeed "combustible."

No one can tell us, beings aware of time that we are, that the world is not interconnected somehow. If we say that nothing "essential" is found in this universe in which we find ourselves, we cannot express this idea without contradicting ourselves. We say at the same time no order or reason exists, then we give a reason for it that we expect others to understand.

Thus, "it is better when a man reads a book from immediate inclination." "The only thing that pleased me in Cicero's book . . .

was its advice to love wisdom itself, and to search for it, to pursue it, hold it, and embrace it firmly." A book is an artifact which only really exists when it is being read and understood. The book is the intelligibility we encounter when we read and understand and judge its truth. "With tears in her eyes, one of the singers led (the deaf) Beethoven to the edge of the stage where he could see the audience cheering." When we finally leave things to "P-s-m-i-t-h," we have to laugh. The tears and the laughter are signs of our humanity. These signs are preserved for us in books that we read and tell others about because we just cannot keep what is true or moving or sorrowful only to ourselves. Ultimately, this is what a book is about.

Chapter 15

On Learning from Not Having Learned*
Some Later Thoughts on Another Sort of Learning

[Disappointment] occurs when the boy who has been enchanted by *Stories from the Odyssey* buckles down to really learning Greek. It comes when lovers have got
married and begin the real task of learning to live together. In every department of life it marks the transition
from dreaming aspiration to laborious doing.
— C. S. Lewis, from the Second Screwtape Letter.[1]

No man had a more ardent love of literature, or a
higher respect for it than Johnson. His apartment in
Pembroke College . . . was over the Gateway. The en-
thusiasts for learning will ever contemplate it with ven-
eration. One day, while he was sitting in it quite alone,
Dr. Panting, then head of the College . . . overheard him
uttering this soliloquy, in his strong emphatick voice:
"Well, I have a mind to see what is done in other places
of learning. I'll go and visit universities abroad. I'll go
to France and Italy. I'll go to Padua—and I'll mind my
business. For an Athenian blockhead is the worst of all
blockheads."
— From James Boswell's *Life of Johnson*, 1730.[2]

---

*   Lecture given at the Bosque School, Albuquerque, New Mexico, May 8,
     2014. Published on-line, Catholic World Report, June 23, 2014.
1   C. S. Lewis, *The Screwtape Letters* (New York: Macmilllan, 1962), p. 11.
2   *Boswell's Life of Johnson* (London: Oxford, 1931), vol. I, pp. 49–50.

I.

"Bosque" is evidently the Spanish word for a forest. Here in the southwest it refers especially to woods along river bottoms. In this school, the river is the famous Rio Grande. One can speak of being educated in a forest or even, I suppose, of being educated by a forest. Tolkien, who had a special love of trees, used to speak of what the forest taught. Our Scriptural heritage speaks of a "Tree of Knowledge of Good and Evil" with a Garden as the original place of the First Parents. The relation of gardens to parks and forests is an interesting one. I believe that the City of St. Louis has a large "Forest Park," as does Everett, Washington.

In one sense today, we must almost say that all of our national forests spread throughout the country are cared for as large scale gardens and parks. In the middle of Munich Germany, is a lovely park called "the English Garden." We probably have no "forests primeval" left. Even the jungles in Brazil come under governmental control. We go out of our way to prevent development of certain woods and lands. In a way, nature becomes more nature when it comes under the scope of human understanding. Nature was not meant simply to be nature. It was also meant to be understood as nature. The things of nature have their own intelligibility.

A school in a forest setting is designed, in the first place, to be a school, not a forest. This particular school was founded in 1994, so it is a mere twenty years old. Its first graduates are still not nearly into what Cicero called "old age." The state in which this school is located is not in "Old" but in "New" Mexico. New Mexico entered the Union on January 6, 1912. My father was born in Iowa in 1904. In the beginning, I cited a passage from James Boswell writing in 1730. This was forty-six years before the signing of the Declaration of Independence and one hundred and twenty-seven years after the founding of Jamestown, Virginia in 1607. I taught in a university in Rome founded in 1551. The usual date given for the founding of the City of Rome is 753 B. C. Thus, in terms of Roman dating, this year, 2014 A.D., is listed as *Ab Urbe Condita*

2767. That is, from the founding of the City of Rome, two thousand seven hundred and sixty-seven years.

I used to insist that students knew, among others, the dates of the deaths of Socrates, Aristotle, Cicero, Augustine, and Aquinas. From the time of Abraham to the time of Socrates was approximately eight hundred years. From the time of Socrates (d. 399 B.C.) to the death of Augustine (d. 430 A.D.) was another eight hundred years; from Augustine to Aquinas was eight hundred years (1274 A.D.). From Aquinas to our days is likewise about eight hundred years. These are time sequences and dates that anyone can remember from early youth if he but learns them. They serve to give some time proportion and structure to our history. We also know of ancient Chinese, Hindu, and Inca calendars. The age of the universe itself is said to be around 13.7 billion years. We like to know what went on, where, and involving whom.

Some education in time and space statistics, in history and geography, is appropriate to the young whose memories are still alert. It is good to know the wheres and whens of things. If we do not take the trouble to know what happened in time and space, we will not be able to place things in relation to each other. Everything will come together as if time and space were collapsed into one blurry time and one fuzzy place. Knowledge of times and places is not the most profound kind of learning. But it provides the context and arena for what are the highest things. Again, I mention this point here as such things are best learned when we are young. We do not waste our time when we know more than our own time and place.

But can we not just look up times and places on our cell phone? No one needs to remember anything. The machine will do it for us. Yet, machines do not know relationships, how the Battle of Hastings in 1066 is related to the Plantagenet House of English monarchs. No machine knows that it knows. Yet, there is too much to remember, no doubt of it. Why not let the machine do it? The machine is a helpful tool to memory, no doubt of it. But if nothing is actually in our heads, we will not see how this relates to that. That is what we have a mind for, to see the connections, the order of things.

And how do we know what we should remember? It is known that 224 different languages are spoken in homes in Los Angeles. If someone knows how to read or if he speaks more than five or six languages, he is doing very well. Doesn't or shouldn't every one speak English or Spanish, even those billions of Chinese and Hindus? Well, no. But some languages are more widely spoken and used than others. All through history there has been the phenomenon of what we call today "English as a second language"—that is, sometimes the main or second language was Greek. That was the result of the conquests of Alexander the Great (d. 323 B.C.). That conquest is the reason the New Testament was originally written in Greek, not Hebrew or Aramaic. But after the Romans conquered much of Africa, Asia, and Europe, Latin became the common language of use. When we speak Spanish or English today, we are using, for the most part, a dialect of Latin, though English also has a lot of German in it.

Am I suggesting that you go out and learn two hundred and twenty-four languages so that you can get along everywhere in Los Angeles? Obviously not. But I am suggesting that you had better learn to read, write, and speak at least one language really well, and it would help to learn a couple more. You can begin to do this in a school in the bosque, in the forest, but only if you will, only if you want to, only if you work at it. Many people with little education learn languages just because they want to or need to. But knowing how to speak a language and knowing how to write it and knowing its literature are much more difficult, but usually, at some point, become delightful projects.

That was the point in the beginning of citing the passage from *The Screwtape Letters* about the young man who was enchanted with stories from Homer's *Odyssey*—a good thing—but he found out that to read the Homeric tales properly, he had to learn Greek. And learning Greek was hard work—not impossible, but not always easy. Yet, unless he learned Greek, the young man was not "free" to read Homer. As in so many things, as in tennis or golf, for example, we are not really "free" to play the game unless we go through the difficulty of learning how to play well.

No one is likely ever to have told us that much of learning is not IQ or native intelligence but will power, docility, the capacity to be taught. We need the will to discipline ourselves, to find good teachers, to follow instructions. We need the will to give up things so that we have time to do what is important. Where are we going to find the time to learn all that we need or want to learn?

I once heard the story of an old Indian woman. Someone was complaining to her that he did not have enough time. She looked at him for a moment and replied: "You have all the time there is." This is one of the things that I want to tell you this evening: you do have all the time there is. We are all busy about many things. Our lives in this world pass within finite limits. It is said that, even though every fact is at our fingertip, we spend much time, as it were, horizontally, not vertically. That is, we spend much time on various electronic devices talking to each other about I know not what.

And one of the things that I will want to tell you this evening is that talking to our friends, while a good thing, improves in quality when we know what things are most important to talk about. Chatter, bantering, and vague musings have their places, no doubt, but they are not what we really mean by conversing about the highest things. For this latter endeavor, you need to read, think, study, pray, write, and experience life.

Again where do we find the time? I like to recommend the book of the Western novelist, Louis L'Amour, called *The Education of a Wandering Man*. This book is an account of how L'Amour found the time to read. He read his way through the history of the old West, its geography, Indians, hills, guns, animals, wars, and lore. He showed how everyone has many moments when he could read if he wanted to or disciplined himself to do so. In what would normally be called "free" time or "down" time, he read many books, the titles of which he recorded in his book. No book, with the possible exception of Sertillanges' *The Intellectual Life*, is quite so useful in explaining to us how much time we have if we pay attention to the details of our daily lives.

II.

This chapter is entitled "On Learning from Not Having Learned."
Another version of the same idea would be that we can "learn from
our mistakes." But here I have something a little different in mind.
It is quite possible to have many academic degrees but still not really be well-educated. It is possible to read widely, but not to have
read well. I might call what I have in mind "remedial liberal arts,"
but still that is not quite the point either.

What I have in mind is an aspect of a larger project that I have
called "Another Sort of Learning." On one of my early walks when
I had first arrived in Washington to teach, I went by a bookstore
on L Street. Seemingly by chance, I went in. I saw a shelf of remain-
ders for sale, mostly paperback books. In those days, I was busy
fleshing out my own personal library, something I recommend as
basic in learning. Not Kindle, not IPads, but books, your books,
things you can hold and mark as you read. In this sense, I am still
a fan of used book stores where often the wisdom of the ages is
available for a relatively modest price if you know what you are
looking for. In this store, I came across a book of the British-Ger-
man economist, E. F. Schumacher. The book was called *A Guide
for the Perplexed*.

I had read Schumacher's well-known book, *Small Is Beautiful*,
but I had never heard of this one, at least by Schumacher. The title
is the same as that of a book of the famous medieval Jewish
philosopher, Moses Maimonides. Just why Schumacher chose this
already famous title was intentionally provocative. So, as a kind of
act of faith, I bought the book and read it. I was astonished by this
short book. Indeed, I have noticed how often the best books are
the short ones—though not always, of course, I know about long
Russian novels. I have recommended *A Guide for the Perplexed*
and assigned it many times over the years since I first bought in
1978.

Schumacher recalled that the "perplexed" in the Middle Ages
were those Jews, Muslims, and Christians who were suddenly con-
fronted with the works of Aristotle finally reaching them from the

East. They had their own books of revelation, but did not realize the extent of what Aristotle knew by the use of his own mind. So they had to relate reason to revelation, lest they be incoherent enough to hold, as some did, that both reason and revelation could be true even if they contradicted each other. This, of course, is impossible. What we know as a university actually came out of this background—*universitas*: "How do all things fit together in a coherent whole?"

What I am concerned about this evening is mostly the first chapter of this short, most illuminating book. Schumacher had been a young teen-age German in an English detention camp during World War II. When old enough, he matriculated at Oxford University, then generally held to be the premier university in the world. But as he, a no-doubt precocious young man, studied there, he was increasingly upset and perplexed. While he was doing well as a student in the subjects actually taught—Schumacher was an economist—he had the growing feeling that little of real human importance was actually being taught or discussed in his studies.

Everything seemed to be based on a reductionist methodology that somehow filtered out any serious discussion of what could not be measured. Schumacher knew that the origin of this reductionist approach had to do largely with Descartes, usually said to be the founder of modern philosophy. But most of what is really important to us, as human beings, is not quantifiable. It must be reached by other philosophical approaches; his education seemed of little value to him. In other words, he realized that he had to look elsewhere for guidance and insight into those areas of reality that most concerned our kind. This little book was the result of his experience. It is astonishing how it matches the academic experience of so many other well-degree-ed people.

III.

As a young man, I had a similar experience. I had been to a semester of college. World War II was just over. I found myself in the army at the Engineering School, then located at Fort Belvoir,

Virginia. We had some free time. Somehow, I had not read much in high school, even with getting pretty good grades. Still the time at Santa Clara gave me the feeling that I was missing something. I needed to read. So I recall going into the Post Library one evening. It was a fairly large, but modest military post library.

As I looked about, I suddenly realized that I had no idea *what* to read, even when I realized that I should read. I knew that you did not just pick up any old book, or begin with the letter A and work your way to Z—that library was still in the Dewey Decimal System of classifying books. No one had time enough to read every book in any good library, even in a long lifetime. Besides, knowledge seemed to have some sort of elusive order to it that I did not understand. Some things were more important than others. Indeed, unless you had read certain things—Plato and Scripture, for instance—other things would not be intelligible to you. Maybe it was this order that universities and colleges were originally designed to teach. At least that is what Dorothy Sayers thought in her famous essay, "The Lost Tools of Learning."

Later, I left the army and spent another year at Santa Clara. I had first tried to major in chemistry. My problem was the opposite to that of most students in the class: that is, I could work out the math but not the experiments on which the math was based. I was next in business school. I found it deadly boring. So I joined the Society of Jesus, a kind of leap in the dark. There, among other things, we were given fifteen or so years to read and study, get degrees and, hopefully, some start at wisdom.

But I always had this nagging image of the young man or lady who finds himself in the midst of vast reams of knowledge but no clue of where to begin or what to read. Subsequently, I imagined lots of students in all sorts of colleges in this and other countries who had the same experience as the young Schmacher. They were pretty sure that they were really learning little of what was really important. But they were implicitly told that what they were missing was not important. In addition I had my own experience. So this is the origin of the title of the present lecture: "Learning from Not Having Learned."

In an old *Peanuts*, Lucy is sitting on the floor reading a book. Linus comes up to her, obviously working on his math assignment. He asks her: "Lucy, how much is six from four?"

In the next scene, she looks up at him to tell him: "Six from four? You can't subtract six from four."

As she goes back to her reading, while Linus looks on, she continues: "You can't subtract a bigger number from a smaller number."

But this information makes Linus angry. He yells to a befuddled Lucy: "You can if you're stupid!"[3]

And that is the thought I want to leave you with. We can do many things if we insist in being stupid. But something will always go wrong with them when we accept stupid or false ideas. Our stupidities are also sources of light if we would see where we are wrong.

Yet, it is a first principle, that is, something whose truth is seen in its very statement, that no one really wants to be stupid, not even Linus. He wants the answer. He is just not yet old enough to understand minus numbers. What I call "another sort of learning" is the finding and reading those seminal books that take us to the truth and order of things. No doubt there are many books that do this. I only know a few of them.

But I constantly think of those students in their late teens and early twenties who somehow sense that what they are studying misses some vital element, some insight into the real nature of things. Or I have in mind many folks, who later in life after settling into their jobs and life, have realized that something has been missing in their formal education. I often receive letters or emails from men or women in their fifties who suddenly have some time from busy lives to realize how much they have missed.

But the spirit I want to leave you with is encapsulated in the title of a recent book of mine—*Reasonable Pleasures*. The title of that book is really from Aristotle who pointed out that all of our

3 In Robert Short, *The Gospel according to Peanuts* (Richmond, VA: The John Knox Press, 1965), p. 119.

human activities are endowed by nature with a corresponding pleasure designed, in effect, to enhance and foster the activity in which it exists. And Aristotle pointed out that there is a pleasure proper to thinking. He suggested that if we do not discover this delight in our own experience, we are likely to confuse it with other activities and other pleasures. Indeed there is a true delight in knowing. I have sought out and found many books that make sense, and, at the same time, delight us. These are the sundry book lists that you will always find me proposing.

One final word, in some sense, the most important chapter in *Another Sort of Learning* is the one called: "What a Student Owes His Teacher." Students often tell me that it never occurred to them that they owed anything, not even gratitude, to their teachers. When we are fortunate enough to find a good teacher, he can take us to important things faster than we could make it there by our unguided selves. And remember, our best teachers do not necessarily have to be alive in our time or in our place. It has been my experience from many years of teaching, that the best teachers often lived thousands of years before our time. Plato remains the best in so many ways.

In the beginning, I cited also a passage from Boswell, a book that is itself an education in the highest things, a long book that is best read a few pages a day. Johnson is in Pembroke College. He is overheard in a moment of anguish. He realizes that what he is learning in Oxford is not everything. He had better find out what is going on elsewhere, in Padua, Paris, or Rome. He sums up his realization by the striking phrase "There is no blockhead like an Athenian blockhead." What does this blunt phrase mean? Athens is the great city of the philosophers. It is still the city that represents Intelligence—Jerusalem, Athens, and Rome, revelation, reason, and law. So if all we know is Athens, we know much. But if we think that this is sufficient, we are but "blockheads."

So we think of what L'Amour called "the education of a wandering man." We can, I hope, take as our own that searching for, that wondering about books that explain things to us, the important things, the highest things. Aristotle was right. There is a pleasure in knowing. We really will not "rest," to use Augustine's word, until we know what is to be known and delight in it. Nothing less explains why Schumacher was unsettled at Oxford or why we still want to learn, not having learned so many things from what we did, in fact, learn.

Chapter 16
DOCILITAS*

On Being Invited into the Kitchen of Heraclitus

The classroom splits into three groups: those who are perfectly submissive because their only interest is to get a credit (grade), those who are said to have powerfully critical minds (they already know all the answers), and those described as intelligently teachable."
— Yves Simon, *A General Theory of Authority*.[1]

Seward: "One should think that sickness and the view of death would make more men religious."
Johnson: "Sir, they do not know how to go about it; they have not the first notion. A man who has never had religion before, no more grows religious when he is sick, than a man who has never learnt figures can count when he has need of calculation."
— *Boswell's Life of Johnson*, Monday, April 29, 1783.[2]

Every realm of nature is marvelous; and Heraclitus, when the strangers who came to visit him found him warming himself at the furnace in the kitchen and hesitated to go in, is reported to have bidden them not to be afraid to enter, as even in that kitchen divinities were present, so

---

*   Published in *Utraque Unum*, 2009.
1   Yves Simon, *A General Theory of Authority* (Notre Dame: University of Notre Dame Press, 1980), p. 95.
2   *Boswell's Life of Johnson* (Oxford: Oxford University Press, 1931), vol. I, p. 493.

we should venture on the study of every kind of animal without distaste; for each animal will reveal to us something natural and something beautiful.
— Aristotle, *Parts of Animals*, 645a17–23.

I.

In Cicero, we find the following phrase: "*Docilis ad hanc disciplinam.*" That is, someone is "teachable" in this particular discipline or field. This "teachableness" means 1) that we have done the preparation so that we can be further taught what we do not yet know and 2) that, in addition, we actually seek to know the truth of the matter at hand. We know that we do not know everything. This unknowing is the very condition of our being what we are. It makes us both uncomfortable and excited. It also alerts us to what is there about us to be known. This "wanting" to know is the most important element in the whole intellectual process. It is the sign of our not being, as they humorously say, "brain dead," which can happen while the rest of our organs are functioning normally.

Without this desiring to know, nothing much happens in us. This willingness to know is the one thing that we cannot "give" to someone else, though we might be able to inspire him or even prod him to know by himself. But it also presupposes that we already find ourselves to be beings that are capable of knowing. This capacity is what makes us different. We know that we did not give ourselves this knowing capacity. We have to wonder why we have it. And once we realize that we in fact have it, we want to do something about it. Namely we want to know more fully what it is and what it reveals to us, namely something not ourselves.

Thus, the very first line of Aristotle's *Posterior Analytics* reads: "All instruction given or received by way of argument proceeds from pre-existent knowledge."[3] No teacher ever enters into a class in which no student knows absolutely nothing. He has to find a place in what is commonly known, from which he can begin. From

3   71a1.

what is commonly known, the dialectic can take us to what is not yet known, as Plato taught us.

We often talk about knowing in general. This knowing gets us into the knowledge of forms, of universals. It is one of the lessons about which Plato still teaches us. This knowledge of forms allows us to speak of the many particulars of a species, of how its individual instances are both the same and different from each other. What is curious about existing things of a single genus or species is that the individuals, while having in common their sameness, also differ in some accidental or particular ways. Each exists, but exists differently.

Forms of what-it-is-to-be-man do not walk down the street. Really existing beings do—John, Mary, and George. No two are exactly alike in their sameness. In the case of human beings, their very divergence among themselves within the same species is what gives rise to speech, politics, and a common good that would see the diversity as itself worthy and in need of reconciling itself with the others in the same species. Indeed, we actually begin with others and see ourselves first in relation to and reflectively in counter-distinction from them.

II.

I have always loved the Latin word, "*Docilitas*," the capacity of being taught. It is related to the idea of a gift, of being that sort of being to whom something lovely happens unexpectedly, to whom something is just given. Teachableness implies something beyond IQ or whatever it is that is said to measure one's native intellectual potential. It implies not merely that we have the capacity to know from our nature, but that we also, from within our individual being, desire to know and do something about acquiring knowledge of what we know we do not yet know. Everyone knows of someone with a supposedly high IQ who never did anything with it. He "never achieved his potential," as they say. We may even suspect it of ourselves.

Too, I am leery of "techniques" for learning, as if you can bypass the learning process itself somehow. The reason why we are not interested in something is not because something is wrong with that which is to be known. The something that is wrong is usually in us, the knowers. Chesterton once said, in a memorable sentence, that I have often cited: "There is no such thing as an uninteresting subject; there are only uninterested people." God did not create anything that did not have origins ultimately in His own being.

Passing from not knowing to knowing can be and certainly is "work," but it is the sort of effort that ends, once completed, in delight. The end of such "work," as Aristotle wrote, is leisure, the activity of *what is* at its best. Knowing is being more than we already are while remaining ourselves. It means that we are not deprived of what is not ourselves as we suspected we might be when we realized how little we did know. The mind is capable of knowing all things, while remaining our knowing in our particular being. In fact, this *"capax omnium* is the very definition of mind. It is what opens the solitariness of our own selves to the abundance of the being *that is.*

The word "docility" implies so much. It shifts the focus of our attention from the teacher who presumably does know something to the learner who does not. Its point of view is not the teacher but the one being taught. It implies the aliveness, the eagerness of the not knower. To be "learned," on the other hand, does not mean simply having learned, but being engaged in the very act of knowing. Truth does not exist outside a mind that affirms what it knows to be true. The learned man begins to see the connection of things.

Further, both the teacher and the learner aim at the same thing. They do not aim at one or the other's truth, but seek truth itself. Neither the teacher nor the learner "owns" the truth but both seek it and, once found, rejoice in it. Truth is free and, as Scripture says, makes us free. Freedom does not make truth to be truth, but allows each of us to find it as something we did not make to be what it is. The highest acts of friendship relate to the truth that belongs to neither friend except as what both know in their own souls to be true. The highest act of friendship, as Aristotle says, is precisely this mutual discovery of the highest things which neither made to be what they are.

Evidently, we run into those people who are not capable of being taught because of their attitude toward or purpose in learning itself. Yves Simon suggests two of these latter types. The first is the student who primarily is concerned with grades. A grade is an external measure of comparative accomplishment. It compares the performance of one student, current or past, to another. It compares all students to a standard of excellence. If, however, we suddenly renounce all forms of grading, we will at the same time undermine any real large-scale discipline in learning.

By making all academic performances equal or unimportant, we end up by having no meaning to academic performance. If everyone gets the same grade no matter what he does, everything is thrown back on the student now separated from any teaching that makes a difference in what is learned. At that point, the student lacks the outside criterion that most of us need and find helpful in knowing whether what we know is valid or not. It is one thing to disagree with a given educational standard, but another to eliminate all standards as if there were no difference between the excellent and the shoddy or dubious. This is but another way of saying truth is not falsity.

None the less, we find enormous pressure on grades and comparative grading systems. Harvey Mansfield at Harvard remarked somewhere that he had a two-tiered grading system, one for the external world outside the confines of Cambridge, and one for actual quality of the student's accomplishment. Since everyone at Harvard thinks obviously he deserves an "A," else why would he be there? He assumes, by virtue of his admission, that he is already superior to anyone else in some other institution. Therefore, every student deserves an "A." However, since within any class, some students are in fact better than others, and the purpose of teaching is to select and point this difference out, there is an internal grading system that does not give everyone an "A."

The student concerned with grades confuses the measure with the measured. Clearly, the student who cares nothing for grades is not an ideal either. But the gulf between what is learned and its measure never quite correlates. The important thing is "What did

I learn?" not "What grade did I get for learning it." The grade does remain a check on ourselves as we study, but graduation usually means the day when grades cease and living the truth because we see it begins. We become less dependent on teachers and more dependent on our own knowing of things, including the highest things. This is what adulthood and maturity are about.

Likewise, another kind of distinction needs to be considered. The fact is that some students with less natural ability end up performing better and knowing more than those with higher native qualities. They may take more time, may be more disciplined, more careful. Eventually they prove to be better and more complete, wiser adults. The measure of our intellectual lives is not so much what we learn in college but what we think about along the way until we reach our declining years. The classical authors were not wrong to associate old age with wisdom, though they too understood the dictum: "There is no fool like an old fool."

. Some things like mathematics can probably be better learned in youth because, as Aristotle said, the discipline does not require experience. Experience is not capable of being learned in a book, though the reading of literature can help. This is why Aristotle tells us that particularly ethical and political books are really not ethics or politics themselves. They are at best guide books to aid us to see what goes on in ourselves and in the souls of others in our polities.

III.

In Aristotle's little treatise known as the *Parts of Animals,* we come across a passage that is mindful of the famous admonition in Book X of the *Ethics* about how we should live. "The scanty conceptions to which we can attain of celestial things give us," Aristotle said in the first treatise, "from their excellence, more pleasure than all our knowledge of the world in which we live; just as a half glimpse of persons that we love is more delightful than a leisurely view of other things, whatever their number and dimensions."[4] Here,

4   644b32–35.

Aristotle has no trouble in admitting that our knowledge of "celestial things" is "scanty," but it is not non-existence. Our glance sees something there, a hint of design, perhaps.

Indeed, although we have a more complete knowledge of the world "in which we live," we have, at the same time, knowing both, a sense of how much more there is to know. Put in other terms, both the cosmos and our immediate world have much to teach us if we will but allow ourselves to be taught by them. But this being taught by us itself requires our active seeking, almost as to say that reality provokes mind whose formulation of it is itself required for its completion.

The comparative example that Aristotle gives of our highest activity is of considerable curiosity. He compares this partial knowledge of the cosmos with the "glance" of someone we love, a glance that itself gives us more delight than "a leisurely view of other things." Surely, this is an experience to which almost anyone can relate. It is but another example of Aristotle's sense of the common man. The implication is that both partial glimpses, the one of the world and the one of someone we love, take us to something of much greater delight and wonder.

In the *Ethics*, Aristotle gave us an oft-pondered piece of advice along the same lines. "We must not follow those who advise us, being men, to think of human things, and, being mortal, of mortal things, but must, so far as we can, make ourselves immortal, and sustain every nerve to live in accordance with the best thing in us; for even if it be small in bulk, much more does it in power and worth surpass everything" (1177b1–78a2). We know that we are advised constantly to concern ourselves only with mortal and human things, not divine ones. The latter are, yes, "impractical." It is, none the less, the insufficiency of the human to satisfy us that makes us suspect that we are already in a higher search of *what is*, even in our concern for what we do in the world.

In the *Parts of Animals*, we also read: "All parts of nature are marvelous." We are introduced into Heraclitus' famous kitchen. Even though we too be strangers and hesitate to enter, we are invited in because "divinities" are present there. More than that, even the ugliest animals we are invited to study, because, like the universe itself, we will find in each particular animal we come across something both "natural and something beautiful." Contrary to Parmenides' principle that "only being is," Heraclitus thought that all being "flowed" and "changed." Still he invited us into his kitchen because ultimate things could be found even there. It is perhaps no wonder that, even with most of us, it is the kitchen of our homes and its memories that remind most of us of the divinities and the beauty of things.

Samuel Johnson is asked in 1783 whether sickness and the approach of death should remind the most hardened sinner of religion. He did not think so. We die as we live. We neither learn calculation nor religion unless we prepare for them. The time when we can be docile to something passes in non-learning and non-use. Johnson implies that there comes a time when, through our own choices, we are not capable of being taught. Even what seem to be the most pressing and riveting experiences can pass by before us unnoticed. The fact is, even in our kitchens, we encounter things every day that we do not notice.

It is a mark of Christian theology to maintain that no human existence passes before its own existence un-noticed. This noticing includes both the unborn and the born. This "being noticed" is the other side of Augustine's famous reference to our "restless hearts" in the first lines of his *Confessions*. We are already caught up in reality by the very fact that we exist and did not cause ourselves to be. Our being is already caught up in the question of whether we are docile, capable of receiving from outside of ourselves what we are. The further question then arises: "On so knowing we receive our existence, do we become, once in being, what we are to be?" The first nature is what we are. The second nature is what we are in charge of and responsible for in ourselves, our deeds and makings.

Without this latter drama of what we do with ourselves in the universe and among those we love, there probably would be no need of a universe in the first place. But the universe itself has within it those beings, ourselves namely, who seek to know it and in so knowing it, they come to know themselves. They know that they are here as beings given to be what they are. This initial receptivity of our being marks us as connected with what is more than ourselves. How odd that we are the kind of beings we are.

Our docility is correlative to those we will allow to teach us about ourselves. Not only are we given ourselves, but we are in charge of whom we allow to teach us about ourselves. Yves Simon remarked, in a memorable phrase: "No spontaneous operation of intellectual relations protects the young philosopher against the risk of delivering his soul to error by choosing his teachers infelicitously."[5] That is delicately put.

In most universities of the world, we cannot take as evidence of what we are Scripture and doctrine, even when they seem uncannily to understand what we are. This reference to reason, of course, is the only ground in which Scripture and doctrine should be offered in the university, as Benedict said in the Regensburg Lecture. When we freely cut off any source of knowledge, we are unteachable by it.

Moreover, there is what, in the same lecture, Benedict XVI calls, rightly, *logos*. The reason that wants to make things and the reason that wants to know things, the practical intellect and the theoretical intellect, belong to the same mind in that being who exists in the world and knows he exists there. The truths of revelation, as Aquinas taught, do not contradict those of reason. This is the tie that binds them together.

IV.

In conclusion, we have all heard the expression of "learning the hard way." It is another way of saying that errors also teach us if we will but let them. The ball game has just been lost by another big score. With ball cap on, glove in hand, and head drooping, Charlie Brown walks dejectedly off the field while Lucy, also with

---

5   Yves Simon, *A General Theory of Authority* (Notre Dame: University of Notre Dame Press, 1980), p. 1.

glove and ball cap, grimly watches yet another disaster of which she was a notable contributor, Charlie says out loud, "Another ball game lost, Good Grief!"

In the next frame with Lucy still following him, Charlie exclaims loudly and poignantly: "I get tired of losing . . . . Every thing I do, I lose!"

But as he turns to her, Lucy, perking up, logically says to a surprised Charlie: 'Look at it this way, Charlie Brown. We learn more from losing than from winning."

To which unwelcome thesis Charlie responds with a shout that flips both Lucy and her logic upside-down: "THAT MAKES ME THE SMARTEST PERSON IN THE WORLD!!"[6] Charlie may not be able to pitch a baseball game, but he certainly understands the logic of defeat.

Docilitas is the capacity of being taught, even the lessons of losing. Unlike the angels, perhaps other forms of Heraclitus's "household divinities," we are not given everything from the beginning to make one choice, up or down. Our teachableness is what binds us together. Chesterton said someplace that the difference between a teacher and a mother is that the teacher teaches one thing to a hundred children, while a mother teaches one hundred things to one child. It is the mother who must know everything, who must teach the young scholar, usually in her kitchen, lest he chooses his professor infelicitously.

It was this same Aristotle on much the same point who assured us that:

> This is why we need to have been brought up in fine habits if we are to be adequate students of what is fine and just, and of political questions generally. For the origin we begin from is the belief that something is true, and if it is apparent enough to us, we will not, at this stage, need reason for why it is true in addition; and if we have

---

6   Cartoon in Robert Short, *The Gospel According to Peanuts* (Richmond, VA.: John Knox Press, 1965), p. 101.

this good upbringing, we have the origins to begin from,
or can easily acquire them (1096b4–9).

If we begin by doubting anything is true, we cannot begin at all.
This was Aristotle's point.

We probably won't find religion on our death bed if we do not
already have it. We will find on examination that all animals are
natural and beautiful. It is well if we are eminently teachable. The
smartest person in the world has learned something from his loses.
"All instruction given or received proceeds by way of argument
from pre-existent knowledge." The young scholar should be careful
lest he choose his mentors infelicitously. For the origin we begin
from is the belief that something is true. We must so far as we can
make ourselves immortal and strain every nerve to live according
to the best thing in us. All parts of nature are marvelous. A half
glance of the persons we love is more delightful than a leisurely
view of other things. The "restless hearts" define our being from
its very inception. We are in the world to direct our hearts to the
rest in which they begin, a rest we cannot, ultimately, give ourselves. This is why we are first receivers.

The virtue of *docilitas*, docility, I think, in conclusion reflects
this prior status we have as beings who receive what we are. Having
received it, no doubt, we are to act on what we are. But in every
case, we are helped and guided if we can accept the fact that others
too have sought and known the truth, that we do not "own" it but
receive it as a gift, even when we know it. The docile man and the
courageous man join forces. They are both willing to receive the
highest things; and, on receiving them, to possess them, to stand
for them. All such gifts are ultimately also to be given away. This
is the only way to retain them.

Conclusion
ON THE "FIXING OF OUR GAZE"*

Let me end these reflections on being teachable, on being open to *what is*, by recalling once again the themes that we have encountered. We recall Aristotle and Plato, Augustine, Aquinas, Seneca, Boswell, Chesterton and many others that we have considered. Finally, it comes down to a certain wonder, to a fascination that we exist at all. We first noticed our very being when we realized that something else besides ourselves existed. How could it be that we came to exist without our own choice being its cause? From our very beginning, and indeed the beginning of all things, we suspect that the things we know and live among are first given to us. Only then, when we have what we did not make, can we really "do" or "make" anything.

When college students go to Europe, as many do, I tell them to be sure to send me a card from the amazingly varied places that they visit, usually randomly. Moreover, before they depart, I tell them that, on coming to *Ostia Antica*, the port of Rome, that they should read, preferably out loud, from *The Confessions* of Augustine, the account of the death of his mother, Monica, there in that place.

When they are in the *Foro Romano*, I add, they should read an oration of Cicero. When they travel to Athens, they should read something of Plato or Aristotle or St. Paul. If they make it to St. Andrews in Scotland, they should read from the wondrous accounts of Boswell and Johnson who paused there on their journey to the Western Isles.

Some students, in fact, even follow my erratic advice. As if to remind me that they had not forgotten what they read in class, I

---

* Published in *University Bookman*, Fall, 2008.

received a photo of two young students who were in Florence. They were in *Santa Croce* before the Tomb of Machiavelli. Later, I received a post card from another young student from Atlanta. She was studying in St. Andrew's for the semester. After apologizing that she did not bring the *Prince* with her on her spring travels, she too was briefly in Florence. She thought to send me a post-card of Machiavelli's Tomb. On it are inscribed the famous words: "*Tanto Nomini, Nullum Par Elogium*"—"For such a name, no praise is equal." The date is MDDXXVII, 1527.

As I too had been in Santa Croce where Machiavelli is buried, I knew there was also there what I remembered to be a tomb of Dante in the same Church. I actually do not think the praise of Machiavelli is that "equal." The foundation of our modern civilization, as Machiavelli understood quite well in the fifteenth chapter of his book, is Socrates. It was the standard of Socrates that Machiavelli must eliminate if he was ultimately to rule the souls of young men and young ladies.

Socrates often said, in searing words we do not forget in these pages: "It is never right to do wrong." Machiavelli, the founder of political modernity, claimed this "right" to do wrong when it was "necessary" to achieve his end of retaining power. The death of Socrates, and indeed the death of Christ, are both the price that was paid for upholding that Socratic principle upon which all human dignity and civilization stands.

The young lady from Atlanta, however, not to be outdone, also sent a photo of the statue of Dante just to assure me that she also knew of the sarcophagus, not tomb, of Dante in Santa Croce. I was so pleased at this bemused and vivid response that I went over to my bookshelves. I found a copy of Dante's *Paradiso*. Somewhat following the method of Augustine in the garden of the Villa outside of Milano, I opened the book randomly. The first lines that I saw were these, from the Tenth Canto:

> Looking upon His Son with all that love
> which each of them breathes forth eternally,
> that uncreated, ineffable first One,

has fashioned all these moves in mind and space
in such sublime proportions that no one
can see it and not feel His Presence there.

Look up now, Reader, with me to the spheres,
look straight to that point of the lofty wheels
where the one motion and the others cross,
and there begin to revel in the work
of that great Artist who so loves His art,
His gaze is fixed on it perpetually.[1]

I was so pleased with this amazing passage that I sent it back to the student as a kind of thanks for leading me, though a photo of the Statue of Dante before Santa Croce, to reread this passage of the *Paradiso*.

I thought to myself later: "Isn't it remarkable that the tomb of Machiavelli is found in a church of Florence called precisely *Santa Croce*, the Church of the Holy Cross!" This place was a vivid reminder of the fate of the just man in existing cities, as Glaucon reminded us in the second book of the *Republic. It is never right to do wrong.* "Death is not the worst evil." "No evil can harm a good man." The power of the politician is limited by the *Santa Croce*. Eternal life is not "endless immortality" in this world, as Benedict reminded us in *Spe Salvi*.

If we return to the last line of Dante—"His gaze is fixed upon it perpetually"—we notice that it does not say that the Divine Artist's gaze is on His own inner Trinitarian life, which it is. Rather, it is "fixed" upon His on-going work of Art, that is, on the cosmos itself and the drama of the free beings within it.

We are often struck when we think of our invitation to behold the "Glory of God," and it is a Glory. But we seldom have it pointed out to us that the loving gaze of God is also upon on us, on our words and deeds. Do we hold and act on the adventure that "it is never right to do wrong"? Or do we accept the principle of

---

1   Musa translation.

the Florentine, whose "name no praise is equal," the principle that: "It is sometimes right to do wrong?"

It never occurred to me until this exchange that the postcard could be a form of literature. I think, after the student's card from Florence via St. Andrew's, Atlanta, and Washington, that I may change my estimate. We must, finally, allow ourselves to live by one or the other of these principles: *Tanto Nomini Nullum Par Eulogium* or *His gaze is fixed upon the divine Art perpetually.*

Machiavelli says it is not what we "ought" to do but what we "do" do that counts. But what are we to do on realizing that the object of the divine gaze is precisely our world? Dante's response to us is simply astounding. We are literally to "begin to revel" in this same work that the great Artist gazes upon. The "beholding" of this same Artist reminds us that we too are made for joy.

The adventure of our existence is stretched out through the heavens, "in mind and space," to allow us to see it, if we will. The *Paradiso* is not possible without the shadow of the *Inferno*. We are to love what the divine Artist loves. No wonder Machiavelli is buried in *Santa Croce*. His effort to teach the potential philosophers, who also read Socrates, need not obscure the gaze of those who see in the Good that completes justice that it is so beautiful. This is why, as Dante says, we "revel" in it.

The virtue of "docility" asks: "Are we are capable of being taught by all things, especially by the highest things?" In the end, we stress the "being capable of being taught," rather than the ability to teach, though that too is a fine art. We are first those who learn what we do not know. The ultimate meaning of our existence is not in our hands or minds. But it is within our grasp if we allow ourselves first to be "teachable," to be willing to listen to what is revealed to us. Only when we are first docile, teachable, taught do we really begin to think. Of such is our being human.

Appendix
FIFTEEN BOOKS TO BE TAUGHT BY

1) A. D. Sertillanges, *The Intellectual Life* (Washington: The Catholic University of America Press, 2008).

2) C. S. Lewis, *An Experiment in Criticism* (Cambridge: Cambridge UniversityPress, 1961).

3) Sean Steel, *The Pursuit of Wisdom and Happiness in Education* (Albany: SUNY Press, 2013).

4) Robert Sokolowski, *Christian Faith & Human Understanding* (Washington: The Catholic University of America Press, 2006).

5) Louis L'Amour, *The Education of a Wandering Man* (New York: Random House, 2008).

6) *Joseph Pieper—an Anthology* (San Francisco: Ignatius Press, 1989).

7) G. K. Chesterton, *What's Wrong with the World* (San Francisco: Ignatius Press, 1994).

8) Christopher Derrick, *Liberal Education as If the Truth Really Mattered* (San Francisco: Ignatius Press, 2001).

9) E. F. Schumacher, *A Guide for the Perplexed* (New York: Harper Colophon Books, 1977).

10) Robert Reilly, *Surprised by Beauty,* (Washington: Morley Books, 2002).

11) John Henry Newman, *The Idea of a University* (Washington: Regnery, 1999).

12) Chantal DelSol, *Icarus Fallen* (Wilmington: ISI Books, 2003).

13) J. M. Bochenski, *Philosophy—an Introduction* (New York: Harper Torchbooks, 1972).

14) Dorothy Sayers, *The Whimsical Christian* (New York: Macmillan, 1978).

15) James V. Schall, *On the Unseriousness of Human Affairs* (Wilmington: ISI Books, 2001).

ABOUT THE AUTHOR

James V. Schall, S.J. is a Professor Emeritus from Georgetown University, where he taught in the Department of Government from 1978–2012. Currently he resides at the Sacred Heart Jesuit Center, in Los Gator, California. He has written essays and columns in various academic and opinion journals. Among his books are: *Another Sort of Learning*; *Political Philosophy & Revelation*; *Remembering Belloc*; *At the Limits of Political Philosophy*; *The Regensburg Lecture*; *Idylls & Rambles*; *The Modern Age*; *On the Unseriousness of Human Affairs*; *Reason, Revelation, and the Foundations of Political Philosophy*; *The Mind That Is Catholic*; *The Classical Moment*, and *The Order of Things*.